AF806906

Zicklin School of Business Financial Markets Series

Robert A. Schwartz, Editor
Zicklin School of Business
Baruch College/CUNY
New York, NY, USA

More information about this series at http://www.springer.com/series/7133

Robert A. Schwartz • John Aidan Byrne
Eileen Stempel
Editors

Market Integrity

Do Our Equity Markets Pass the Test?

Springer

Editors
Robert A. Schwartz
Zicklin School of Business
Baruch College/CUNY
New York, NY, USA

John Aidan Byrne
Rockaway, NJ, USA

Eileen Stempel
Zicklin School of Business
Baruch College/CUNY
New York, NY, USA

Zicklin School of Business Financial Markets Series
ISBN 978-3-030-02870-1 ISBN 978-3-030-02871-8 (eBook)
https://doi.org/10.1007/978-3-030-02871-8

Library of Congress Control Number: 2018963829

© Springer Nature Switzerland AG 2019
This work is subject to copyright. All rights are reserved by the Publisher, whether the whole or part of the material is concerned, specifically the rights of translation, reprinting, reuse of illustrations, recitation, broadcasting, reproduction on microfilms or in any other physical way, and transmission or information storage and retrieval, electronic adaptation, computer software, or by similar or dissimilar methodology now known or hereafter developed.
The use of general descriptive names, registered names, trademarks, service marks, etc. in this publication does not imply, even in the absence of a specific statement, that such names are exempt from the relevant protective laws and regulations and therefore free for general use.
The publisher, the authors, and the editors are safe to assume that the advice and information in this book are believed to be true and accurate at the date of publication. Neither the publisher nor the authors or the editors give a warranty, express or implied, with respect to the material contained herein or for any errors or omissions that may have been made. The publisher remains neutral with regard to jurisdictional claims in published maps and institutional affiliations.

This Springer imprint is published by the registered company Springer Nature Switzerland AG
The registered company address is: Gewerbestrasse 11, 6330 Cham, Switzerland

Preface

The Low Down on High Intraday Volatility

Opening Remarks

Robert A. Schwartz
Zicklin School of Business, Baruch College, CUNY
New York, USA

"What is the meaning of integrity" is the focus of today's conference. We certainly know what integrity implies, but actually defining the word is not an easy matter. I Googled and soon learned that integrity has to do with consistency as well as truthfulness and accuracy. I will accept that from Google and will also add reliability just for good measure.

To start, I would like to focus on accuracy. So, where, you are asking, am I heading? Straight to price discovery, something that I have previously talked about here at our annual Baruch conferences. Today, we have two panels focused on price discovery. The first, from the perspective of the exchanges, is moderated by Justin Schack; and the second, moderated by Ian Domowitz, is from the perspective of the customers. Price discovery is an excellent lead into intraday volatility, something I also wish to focus on today in my introductory remarks.

I emphasized the importance of good price discovery in my opening remarks for the 2011 conference, "The Economic Function of a Stock Exchange." While editing my remarks for the 2011 conference book published by Springer,[1] I saw the basis of a strong and persuasive paper, so I invited my doctoral student, Nazli Sila Alan, to co-author it with me. Our efforts have resulted in a paper, Price Discovery: The

[1] Springer, Part of Springer Science+Business Media.

Economic Function of a Stock Exchange, published in the Fall 2013 issue of the *Journal of Portfolio Management (JPM).*[2]

Price discovery, in my opinion, has received insufficient attention. How come? It is complex and not well understood. More importantly, it is very hard to measure. How might one assess the accuracy of price discovery vis-à-vis underlying equilibrium values, which is something we love to talk about in our economics courses? Where do the aggregate buy and sell curves cross to describe a broad market's desire to hold shares in equity trading? God only knows. For us mortals, equilibrium prices are simply not observable.

Can a benchmark be used to infer the inaccuracy of price discovery? Yes, this is possible. To obtain this benchmark, let me introduce the concept of price discovery noise. Price discovery noise, which refers to the deviations of actual prices from equilibrium values, is manifest in an accentuation of intraday price volatility. Intraday volatility is, of course, accentuated, as we all know, by spreads and market impact. But I submit that the noise is largely attributable to prices dynamically searching for, and not easily attaining, equilibrium values. From the data we accessed, it certainly appears to be the case in the opening moments of trading and for the first half hour of trading. The main reason for the accentuated volatility which we and many others have observed in the data (and many of you have observed in reality) comes not from spreads, not from market impact, but from inaccuracies in price discovery. To see this, let's look at some stats from my JPM paper with Sila.

To obtain a volatility measure on a daily basis, we assess high/low spreads expressed as a percent. In doing so, we have sorted all of the US stocks in each and every trading day in 2011, according to their opening volatility, into 20 equally sized groups for each individual stock. Today, I want to focus on a subset of these stocks: Just the big ones, the Dow Jones Industrial Average (DJIA) stocks between \$30 and \$100 in prices. For each of these groups as shown in Table 1, we can have several Dow stocks. We simply selected the highest Dow stock in each group, and that stock is identified on the left. Our purpose was to find the more striking situations, the more volatile situations. A large number is in the eyes of the beholder. Our lowest observation was 0.33% on April 6, 2011, in Johnson & Johnson (JNC). The highest was Disney (DIS). We were looking for special cases like this.

Consider Disney (DIS) in Table 1, on August 10, with a volatility of 7.61% observed for Disney. This number is the percentage difference between the high price in that half hour and the low price at which Disney traded. So 7.61% means that, within a half-hour period, somebody bought at a price 7.61% greater than somebody else paid for the stock. Somebody sold higher and somebody sold lower. Is that integrity or hypocrisy? What's going on?

[2] "Price Discovery: The Economic Function of Stock Exchange," by Nazli Sila Alan and Robert A. Schwartz was published in The Journal of Portfolio Management Fall 2013, 40 (1) 124–132; DOI: https://doi.org/10.3905/jpm.2013.40.1.124

Table 1 Opening volatility selected Dow stocks

Company name (ticker)	Date	Avg price	Hi-Lo	Spread	Volatility (%)	Adjusted volatility (%)	Group[a]
Johnson & Johnson (JNJ)	04/06/11	$59.82	$0.20	$0.01	0.33	0.31	5
Boeing (BA)	06/29/11	$72.34	$0.38	$0.03	0.53	0.49	6
Home Depot (HD)	04/20/11	$38.34	$0.25	$0.01	0.65	0.62	7
Merck (MRK)	09/27/11	$32.06	$0.25	$0.01	0.78	0.74	8
Travelers Companies (TRV)	08/04/11	$53.32	$0.48	$0.02	0.90	0.86	9
Exxon Mobil (XOM)	05/26/11	$81.92	$0.82	$0.01	1.00	0.99	10
Procter & Gamble (PG)	04/12/11	$62.52	$0.71	$0.01	1.14	1.12	11
McDonalds (MCD)	10/05/11	$86.19	$1.12	$0.04	1.30	1.26	12
Walmart (WMT)	01/20/11	$55.66	$0.80	$0.01	1.44	1.41	13
American Express (AXP)	09/26/11	$46.59	$0.77	$0.03	1.65	1.60	14
United Technologies (UTX)	02/24/11	$82.74	$1.53	$0.03	1.85	1.81	15
Unitedhealth Group (UNH)	12/08/11	$49.25	$1.05	$0.02	2.13	2.08	16
Verizon (VZ)	08/01/11	$35.80	$0.89	$0.01	2.49	2.46	17
Du Pont (DD)	08/05/11	$47.88	$1.45	$0.02	3.03	2.99	18
Jpmorgan Chase (JPM)	08/25/11	$37.69	$1.57	$0.01	4.17	4.14	19
Disney (DIS)	08/10/11	$30.34	$2.31	$0.02	7.61	7.55	20

[a]There are no Dow stock observations in the first four groups, therefore our table starts from Group 5

There was no news announcement at the time. We plotted the price movements over this half-hour period. It was indeed an uncertain time in the market. Markets were profoundly rattled by the European debt crisis. Could that explain it? Not so easily, Disney opened at the high price is what happened. How accurate was that price? How accurately did that price reflect the underlying propensities of investors to hold shares? Was the opening price produced by the intersection of a buy curve – call it like a demand curve, and a sell curve – call it like a supply curve? Disney's opening price was an equilibrium price that intersection would have delivered. But it is not easy to find an equilibrium price when investors have different opinions about share values.

Much of the various works by Sila and I and some others of us here is in the context of investors having what we call "divergent expectations." That conflicts with a lot of what's taught in standard academic courses and its opposite homogenous expectations, underlies many academic models (e.g., the capital asset pricing model). If investors have homogeneous expectations, then you don't need a marketplace to

Table 2 Price paths: DIS & SPY on 8/10/11 9:30AM–10:00AM

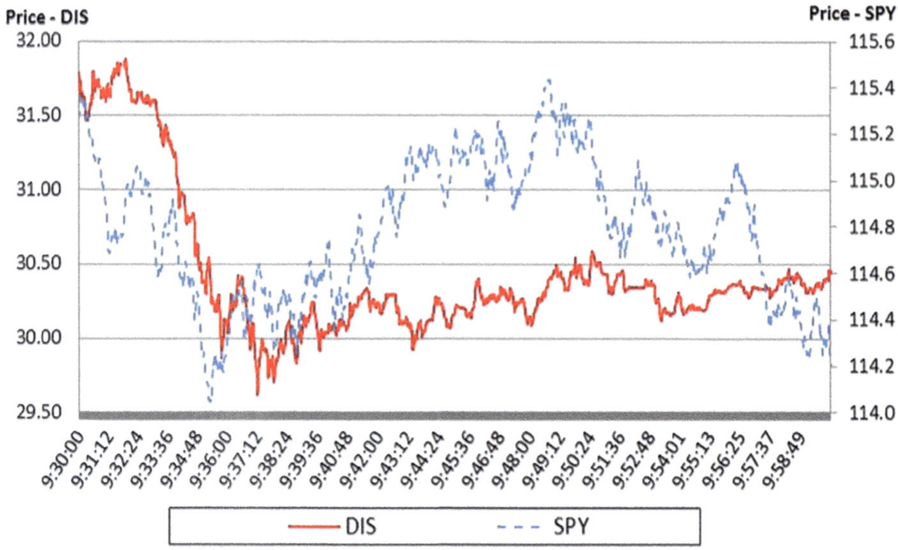

find the value of shares of a stock. We just know what it is. The research analysts know what it is. But when they have divergent expectations, this knowledge about an equilibrium price disappears.

In times of stress such as in August of 2011 with the European debt crisis flaring, we certainly expect that expectations were more diverse across investors, and so price discovery was harder to determine. Now look at Table 2. The red line is Disney, and the dotted darker line is SPDR S&P 500 ETF (SPY), so you can relate to what else is going on in the market. They're fairly correlated. Disney opened too high, then it went higher, and then it goes down. Why? What accounts for it? Is it because something happened in those minutes, because the initial price was not a good price, or because it lacked integrity? I think it's the latter. This is in my paper with Sila, and it's an important way of looking at things. Now let's take the full set of Dow stocks. Let's get away from Disney and look at the opening half hour in each stock day. Every day we look at every stock and get its high/low. In Table 3, we group the stocks into volatility groups. The same stock can be in different groups on different days. I didn't say it with the previous slide, but I'll say it here because it's the same thing. Why do the groups begin at group 5 down to group 20? Because no Dow stocks were in groups 1 through 4, they all have higher volatility.

What we're looking at is this: One stock can be in different groups on different days, it doesn't matter. For each group, we show the average high/low, the minimum and maximum volatilities, and the number *(N)* of observations in a group. What's interesting is that 43% of the observations fall into the higher groups, 11 through 19, the percentage is pretty low for group 20. Lo and behold (no pun intended), volatil-

Table 3 DOW stocks: opening volatility by Vol Group, 252 trading days in 2011

Group[a]	Mean (%)	Median (%)	Min (%)	Max (%)	N[b]	% N (%)
5	0.28	0.28	0.16	0.31	77	1.02
6	0.42	0.42	0.32	0.49	607	8.03
7	0.56	0.56	0.49	0.62	939	12.42
8	0.68	0.68	0.62	0.74	1032	13.65
9	0.80	0.80	0.75	0.86	854	11.30
10	0.92	0.92	0.87	0.99	780	10.32
11	1.05	1.05	0.99	1.12	754	9.97
12	1.18	1.18	1.12	1.26	600	7.94
13	1.33	1.33	1.26	1.42	503	6.65
14	1.50	1.49	1.42	1.60	412	5.45
15	1.70	1.70	1.60	1.81	294	3.89
16	1.94	1.93	1.81	2.09	259	3.43
17	2.25	2.24	2.09	2.46	197	2.61
18	2.71	2.68	2.46	3.02	148	1.96
19	3.49	3.40	3.03	4.14	78	1.03
20	5.56	4.86	4.19	8.89	26	0.34

[a]There are no Dow stock observations in the first four groups, therefore our table starts from Group 5

[b]Total number of observations is 7560 (30 stocks × 252 trading days)

Table 4 Opening volatility: NYSE & NASDAQ stocks

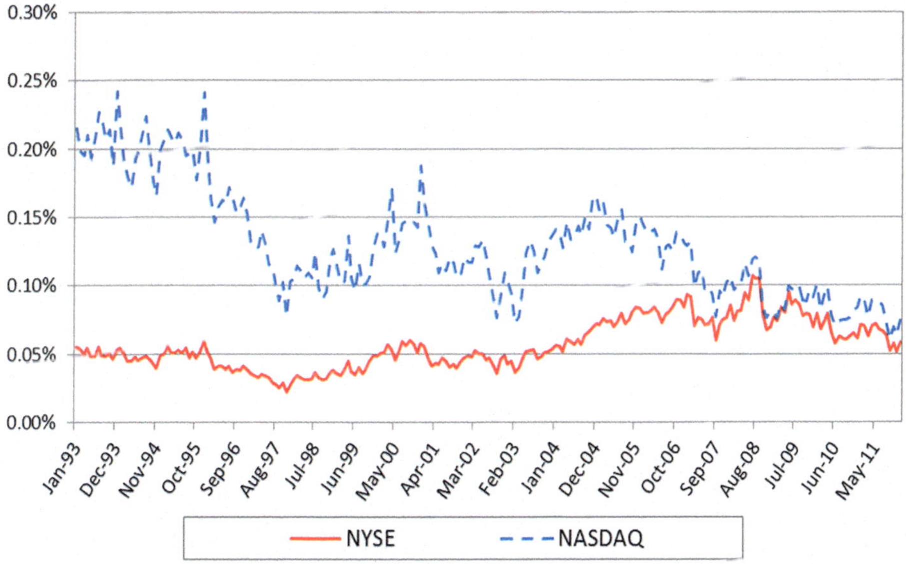

ity for group 20 is huge! For group 11, the volatility was 1.05%, for 19 it was 3.49%. That's the percentage difference between the high and the low price in the first half hour. It's fairly representative of this data. I don't know what you are thinking, sitting here, looking at it, and I hope our conference today delves into related issues during the day. But it seems pretty striking to me. And that was the purpose of our paper to find out. Gosh, people *talk* about volatility, about it being high and inflated. Sila and I wanted to obtain a succinct read on it.

In Table 4, I will present what has happened over time. Have our markets improved according to this measure of market quality? We look at NASDAQ, and we look at the NYSE – and this is fairly striking to me. Now, the conservative thing to say about NYSE volatility is that it starts a good deal lower, and that it certainly has not decreased. Nice if it had. NASDAQ, for the most part, has come down. There have been big swings on NASDAQ, but it has otherwise dropped down, and the NYSE has risen. What could account for this? I will suggest one factor: fragmentation. We've been looking at this. Sila has looked, and fragmentation really seems to be a cause of what I have described. Over time the NYSE market, as we all know, has fragmented. It's gone from over 80% of market share of trading in its own listed stocks to under 30% by some measures under 30%, and it is now in the 20% range. HFT has affected NASDAQ as well as the NYSE, and we have somewhat more direct evidence elsewhere. But it's not so easy to pull together all the relevant evidence. Enough said. I do know one thing, it gives me great pleasure to welcome you here today. Let's discuss all of this.

List of Participants

Name	Company	Title
Joe Bonocore	Citigroup	Managing Director and Deputy Treasurer
Andrew Brooks	T. Rowe Price Associates, Inc.	Vice President and Head of U.S. Equity Trading
Eric Budish	Booth School of Business - University of Chicago	Associate Professor of Economics and William S. Fishman Faculty Scholar
Bryan Christian	Direct Edge	Head of Sales
Colin Clark	NYSE Euronext	Senior Vice President, Strategic Analysis
Deanna Dobrowsky	IIROC	Vice-President, Regulatory
Ian Domowitz	ITG Solutions Network and ITG, Inc.	CEO and Managing Director, respectively
John Donahue	Fidelity Capital Markets	Senior Vice President, Head of Equity
Huseyin Erkan	World Federation of Exchanges	CEO
Tom Gira	FINRA	Executive Vice President and Head of Market Regulation
Frank Hatheway	NASDAQ OMX Group, Inc.	Chief Economist
Gary Katz	International Securities Exchange	President & CEO
John Kelly	Liquidnet	Chief Operating Officer
Ken Lehn	Katz Graduate School of Business - University of Pittsburgh	Samuel A. McCullough Professor of Finance
William Lishman	Schroeders	Head of Equity Trading Americas
Timothy Mahoney	BIDS Trading	CEO
Lin Peng	Baruch College	Associate Professor
Bob Pisani	CNBC	Correspondent
Keith Ross	PDQ Enterprises LLC	CEO

(continued)

Name	Company	Title
Justin Schack	Rosenblatt Securities	Managing Director, Market Structure Analyst
Robert Schwartz	Zicklin School of Finance, Baruch College	Speiser Professor of Finance
Adam Sussman	Tabb Group	Partner, Director of Research
Eric Swanson	BATS Global Markets, Inc.	General Counsel
Lee Van Slyke	Extraordinary Re Holdings, Inc.	President
Steve Wunsch	Wunsch Auction Associates, LLC	CEO

Conference Sponsors

BATS Exchange
BIDS Trading
Bloomberg Tradebook LLC
Chicago Board of Options Exchange
Deutsche Börse AG
Direct Edge
International Securities Exchange
ITG Inc.
Liquidnet
NASDAQ OMX
NYSE Euronext
PDQ ATS Inc.
TABB Group

Contents

Chapter 1
Integrity of Price Discovery: Perspective of Exchanges

Justin Schack, Bryan Christian, Colin Clark, and Frank Hatheway

Justin Schack: We listened earlier to Professor Schwartz talking about price discovery and the noise associated with this phenomena.[1] In his presentation, Bob cleverly probed our market structure for the changes that have potentially led to a degradation in market quality. An academic paper about this same issue has taken a slightly different tack by looking at quote activity. In particular, it looked at quote activity in the wake of the market access rule that went into effect in 2011 in response to the Flash Crash,[2] a rule which basically banned naked market access.[3] I want to talk briefly about the findings and ask Frank Hatheway, as an academic, to respond. The paper found that quoting activity went down

As of writing in 2016, Bryan Christian is senior vice president, head of US sales at Bats Global Markets, a role that reflects the completion of the merger between Bats and Direct Edge in early 2014.

[1] See Preface: The Low Down on High Intraday Volatility". Robert Schwartz, Speiser Professor of Finance, Zicklin School of Business, Baruch College, CUNY. Professor Robert Schwartz

[2] The Flash Crash of May 6, 2010, lasted about 36 min, erasing 998.5 points, or about 9% in the Dow Jones Industrial Average, and then quickly recouping the losses as the various indexes rapidly rebounded in these high-speed, electronic trading phenomena. At the time, it was a record 1-day point decline on an intraday basis in the history of Dow Jones Industrial Average.

[3] The Securities and Exchange Commission adopted the final version of Rule 15c3-5 on November 3, 2010. See Risk Management Controls for Brokers or Dealers with Market Access. Securities and Exchange Commission. https://www.sec.gov/rules/final/2010/34-63241.pdf

J. Schack (✉)
Rosenblatt Securities, New York, NY, USA

B. Christian
Direct Edge, Jersey City, NJ, USA

C. Clark
NYSE Euronext, New York, NY, USA

F. Hatheway
The NASDAQ OMX Group, Inc., New York, NY, USA

© Springer Nature Switzerland AG 2019

R. A. Schwartz et al. (eds.), *Market Integrity*, Zicklin School of Business Financial Markets Series, https://doi.org/10.1007/978-3-030-02871-8_1

substantially but that market quality improved at the same time with the rate of cost going down by 10%. This suggests that there may be some elements in our market structure today that are somehow leading to less market quality. Frank, would you lead us off?

Frank Hatheway: At the end of the day, we are all striving to preserve the investors' alpha. These investors are the client. Preserving alpha depends on supply and demand and on the markets sending an accurate price signal. And another part of preserving alpha is that the price impact of a trade should only reflect the incremental change in supply and demand from that trade. There should be as little frictional price impact as possible. There is tension between accurate price signals and on minimizing the price impact of a trade. Every opaque order we have, every step we take to reduce price impact, flickering quotes, and other aspects of how the market works, reduces the information about supply and demand. There is this trade-off between price discovery, information about supply and demand, and price impact. And whether that is all good or bad is a complex question. Bob's study, and the separate paper you were alluding to, Justin, by Bidisha Chakrabarty, shows different views from the academic community on these issues.[4] I don't think anyone believes the price behavior in Disney shares in August of 2011 is what we strive for.[5] What happened to the alpha of different sets of investors trying to trade during that whole experience or other similar events that take place in the market? Academic research can take a diagram like that for Disney, a 1-day pattern in one stock a few years ago, and move it from an anecdote, and look at 18 years of data. Examine the last graph that Bob [Schwartz] put up in his presentation this morning, and notice price volatility during the first half hour of the trading day, across 18 years on the two markets.[6] You can see some fairly clear or very clear trends emerging. We can certainly get into a big argument about why and the causes.

The Chakrabarty paper looks at one event in the fourth quarter of 2011. There was a hell of a lot of other things happening in 2011, so it is hard for that paper to be definitive. The authors do as good a job as they possibly could. But there are constraints when you have a one-time event and in what you can say about it. There are other researchers who will look at that study and see what insights can be drawn from a broader sample of events. We heard talk about obfuscation today. Well, I would like to rephrase that, if I can, as we think about the balance of this panel. We are really concerned about the way the markets work about transferring alpha from investors to the intermediaries and about whether the way the markets are evolving

[4] See latest, as of writing: Chakrabarty, Bidisha and Jain, Pankaj K. and Shkilko, Andriy and Sokoloy, and Konstantin. *Speed of Market Access and Market Quality: Evidence from the SEC Naked Access Ban* (May 16, 2014). Western Finance Association 2014; 28th Australasian Finance and Banking Conference. Available at SSRM, http://ssrn.com/abstract=2328231 or http://dx.doi.org/10.21.39/ssrn.2328231

[5] See Preface: The Low Down on High Intraday Volatility – Robert Schwartz. Speiser Professor of Finance, Zicklin School of Business, Baruch College, CUNY.

[6] Ibid.

increases or decreases that transfer. In Bob's chart on Disney, if it is the intermediaries who are selling high and buying low, it is a very different story than if it is different classes of investors who are on different sides of those trades.

Colin Clark: Some of the trends are very interesting. On the NASDAQ side, it seems a key factor that was driving intraday volatility down at the open is the introduction of a call market by 2005.[7] More interesting is the period around 2004–2008, when you could see an increase in intraday volatility on New York-listed securities toward the opening. As you think about what happened, you could conclude that it was related to changes in market share. A significant amount of market share shifted away from the NYSE to other electronic markets. There was a significant increase in just electronic trading in NYSE-listed securities. The NYSE itself had introduced electronic trading and was starting to trade more electronically by 2006.[8] Finally, New York lists a lot of financial stocks, proportionally more than NASDAQ. That also could have had an impact over that period, particularly heading into 2007 and 2008, within the time frame of the global financial crisis.

Schack: Is fragmentation, as Bob suggested in his opening speech, an issue here? In other words, we have 13 US exchanges today, and that's quite a few more than several years ago. We have, depending on who you ask, 40, 50, or 60 or more ATSs.[9] Our firm thinks there are probably more than a couple dozen that probably do meaningful volume. In any event, it is an awful lot of choice for brokers. Last month, we saw a record for off-exchange trading. It seems like we have been setting records for off-exchange trading on a regular basis so far this year. Now almost 38% of US equities trades are happening away from the display markets.[10]Are we at the tipping point now where it is starting to hurt price discovery?

Hatheway: I will certainly say, yes, we are past it. We're higher than that 38% once you take the auctions out. Over 4000 listed securities are more than 40% dark, in terms of the volume executed over the counter, that's even including the auctions. What is the tipping point? It's where we get, in terms of alpha preservation, less than what we give up in terms of alpha loss. Because price discovery gets worse, the ability to measure price impact deteriorates, and price impact may erroneously appear to get better. The conflation of deteriorating price discovery, and accurately

---

[7] NASDAQ introduced an opening and closing call market in 2004.

[8] The New York Stock Exchange under then CEO John Thain expanded its electronic trading platform by introducing a "hybrid market" in August 2004, a step that combined the manual handling of orders on the floor with greater use of its computerized NYSE Direct system.

[9] A story by John McCrank, published by Reuters, counted 91 ATSs registered with the Securities and Exchange Commission, as of August 1, 2013, with these ATSs trading in various asset classes. See US securities watchdog proposes new rules for "dark pools." John McCrank, *Reuters*, October 1, 2013, http://articles.chicagotribune.com/2013-10-01/news/sns-rt-regulation-darkpoolsfinra-20131001_1_dark-pools-crossfinde

[10] These "display markets" would include the New York Stock Exchange. These markets are "lit" in the classic sense, unlike dark pools where prices are not displayed to investors.

measuring price impact, is a problem that always arises when we get into these debates. Order by order, I can't change the status quo. So the optimal thing for me to do in handling an order may be different than what would be optimal if I could change the status quo about how the market is organized. I assume we'll have the same sorts of arguments here today. Under the status quo, I want to put my trade in a dark pool[11] or into whatever type of system I think is appropriate. That's because I think that's the best way, given the world I have to operate in, to get best execution for my client. On the flipside, what should the world we operate in look like? As Bob's study shows, at least in the first half hour, the market quality we have with respect to volatility isn't as good as the one we might have had or at least used to have on the NYSE side prior to Reg NMS 10 years ago.[12]

Clark: We've been advocating protecting displayed liquidity with some sort of price improvement requirement, or size requirement, for trades in the away markets. In terms of some of your percentages, yes it's 38%, a record level in terms of off-exchange trading. If you look at other pockets of the market, NASDAQ-listed securities are now hitting 42% off-exchange; NYSE-listed securities that are more thinly traded are hitting around 37% or 38% off-exchange.

We support dark trading, to a degree. There's a lot of good behavior in the dark pools.[13] There's a significant amount of meaningful price improvement. There's a significant amount of block activity in the dark. We do have concern with the small-sized orders that are executing at a displayed exchange price with no price improvement. We have looked at the data, and we see evidence of market quality erosion. We've done some cross-sectional analysis, grouping stocks into various volume and price buckets. We've concluded that, within a given bucket, stocks that have higher off-exchange trading have wider spreads. It's a fairly consistent number across buckets.

Bryan Christian: Dark pools are a topic of much industry debate. Ultimately, the discussion here is looking for that smoking gun when it comes to dark pools. Everybody wants data; everybody wants more of the data to prove where dark pools fail us, where exchanges get the advantage. I don't have the answer to that. I do know that transparency is key to this. Just last week, the Chairman of the Securities

---

[11] For a comprehensive account of dark pools and their opposite in lit markets, see *Dark Pools: Fear of the Dark.* Third Way. Lauren Oppenheimer, John Vahey. August 28, 2013. http://www.thirdway.org/report/dark-pools-fear-of-the-dark

As the authors explain: "Dark pools are private, electronic stock trading venues that allow buyers and sellers of a stock to be matched anonymously. In a dark pool, prices are not displayed to investors – stock prices are dark. Dark trading is an alternative to trading on a 'lit' exchange, like the New York Stock Exchange (NYSE), where traders benefit from visible prices."

[12] Reg NMS (Regulation National Market System) was adopted by the Securities and Exchange Commission in 2005 and introduced 2 years later to further advance the ideals of a national market system. The regulation includes the order protection, or trade-through rule, access rule (fair access) to market data including quotations, and rules on sub-penny trading and on market data.

[13] See footnote 12.

and Exchange Commission, Mary Jo White, said the MIDAS system will be coming online.[14] Fragmentation is a reality today. I don't necessarily agree with people who say the rules in the marketplace are not natural. The data will help us prove how we all think the rules have affected our business. And more data will soon be available to more people.[15]

Schack: One of the ways some of the exchanges have tried to cope with this 38% figure is by introducing what have been referred to as Retail Liquidity Programs, or RLPs.[16] Under this plan, they have a special order type, or a special program, that can receive what are designated as retail orders. We think it's about 10–15% of all US volume that is marketable retail flow executed off-exchange and internalized by wholesale market makers.[17] Is that an appropriate and beneficial response? Or, is it just coping with a sub-optimal regulatory structure, a structure where the exchanges can't do what the broker can do, so this is their next best effort? But it's really making things more complex and fragmented?

Clark: There is a key difference in the programs we're introducing. And we've a couple of different programs on the retail side. One is trying to draw in the retail liquidity providers. We are doing that by offering an attractive rebate to get them to post in our venue. With the exception of the rebate, there is no different treatment of that retail order versus any other order, because we value the liquidity. On the flip side, and what Justin is alluding to, we have our Retail Liquidity Program where we're trying to attract retail takers. The lion's share, if not all, of that flow, is traded off-exchange today.[18]

We came up with a creative solution to draw in that liquidity. The results have been mixed. The key point is that it is different than what happens off-exchange.

---

[14] MIDAS, or the Market Information Data Analytics System, captures large amounts of data from the consolidated tapes and proprietary data feeds on Wall Street. The system, which went live in late 2013, is said to collect over one billion records a day.

See Midas: https://www.sec.gov/marketstructure/midas.html.

[15] Referring to MIDAS.

[16] For example, the New York Stock Exchange launched its Retail Liquidity Program in 2012. "The electronic Retail Liquidity Program requires liquidity providers to improve the best protected bid or the best protected offer (PBBO) by a minimum increment, benefitting the retail investor's execution price. Operating similar to a Dutch-auction, executions will occur at the price that completes the transaction. Each transaction will include a rebate for RMOs [Retail Member Organizations] and a fee for RLPs [Retail Liquidity Providers] who interact with the Retail Orders. There is a minimum price improvement requirement of $0.001 and quoting is in increments of $0.001. Stocks priced under $1.00 are not eligible for the Program. The allocation methodology for competing quotes is as follows: *ƒ* Price time ranking *ƒ* But will execute at the price that completes/maximizes executions." Source: NYSE website.

[17] Internalized refers to a trade is internalized for an investor when it is handled and executed by their "internalizing" brokerage firm using securities held by this investor's brokerage. Brokerage firms that internalize orders can sometimes benefit from the spread, in this case, the difference between what they pay for the shares and what they sell them for.

[18] See footnote 17.

A retail liquidity provider has to price improve in order to interact with that retail order; otherwise that retail order will interact with the best displayed price on the market. That's very different than what happens off-exchange, where a retail order can interact with a dark order that's trading at the same price as an exchange.

Schack: It's not surprising to hear exchanges talk about there being too much dark trading. I want to briefly depart from the script and explore the flip side of that. You talked about price improvement, Colin. When you look at the statistics, people are generally doing better by accessing programs like RLPs than they would be by going to a wholesaler. But they are not availing themselves of those programs. Retail brokers, at least, continue to send the vast majority of their flow off-exchange. If they do that, one of the big issues is that you guys can't make them whole if there is an error. When we talk about ways to unpack this crazy package, is that what the equity markets have become?? Is that one of the things you would put on the table in discussions about reforms? Would you say that we would be willing to move on something like that, if it led to our competing on a more level playing field, with a lot of the off-exchange venues, internalizing brokers?[19]

Hatheway: Let me jump in here. That augments complexity by adding another set of rules on top of what might be a sub-optimal set of rules to begin with. This is the way New York dealt with making someone whole, if there was an error in the old days. The trade was between the specialist and the member firm. If a specialist needed to make an accommodation, he or she could do so, and often did. I was a floor guy for 5 years on the options side in Philadelphia, and member accommodation happened there too.[20] You can't readily provide an accommodation in an anonymous electronic limit order book. Exchanges now are the locus of the trade, not the two members. Everything you are proposing now, Justin, says that you, the exchange, is the locus of the trade. We're going to give the exchange flexibility that probably best sits with a broker-dealer, not with an SRO,[21] because an SRO then faces the issue of interacting fairly and consistently with different members. That would be a quick reaction to your suggestion about exchanges being able to make a member whole. There may be better ways to deal with that, with unpacking some of the regulations that are already in place, than by creating another category of regulations that would overlay what we have.

Christian: The Retail Liquidity Program at the NYSE talks about customer segmentation. And the RLP program has provided choices to the Street. Aside from whether it's been successful or not, one thing we do know is that, with fragmentation, industry participants now have more choices. As an exchange, we offer an order type, and people choose to use it or not. Customer segmentation has provided

[19] See explanation on internalization in footnote 18.

[20] Before earning his doctorate in Economics, Dr. Frank Hatheway was a derivatives trader and the president of Hatheway & Company, Inc., a member firm of the Philadelphia Stock Exchange.

[21] Self-regulatory organization.

the exchanges another way to compete. Have we gotten it right? The success, ultimately, will be proven in the products and participation, so we just don't know how it all evolves down the road. I don't really have the answer right now. I do know that the current industry setup provides a way for the exchanges to innovate within the current rule segment. And I agree with Frank concerning the complexity. I will add that, in today's environment, customer segmentation allows exchanges to get innovative again.

Hatheway: I like bringing segmentation into the discussion, but I don't like segmentation as a practice. To me, segmentation is a way to increase intermediation, and intermediation is a friction. It doesn't mean that intermediaries are making more money, because they're in a competitive business themselves. They just start offering more and more services. It creates higher costs and more friction. You get back to the story of where does the alpha go. There are other industries that operate on the principal of establishing a certificate of need, and healthcare being an example. Let me explain: You can't add another hospital in an area where there is no need for it. In the same vein, you can't add an exchange in our context, unless the exchange you propose will either offer something really radically different or will fill an unaddressed niche in the exchange market. That's as opposed to creating a "me too" exchange that simply copies an existing market. Some of the exchanges that have been launched, and probably some of the exchanges that Colin and Bryan have been part of, literally copy a rule book.

Schack: Someone mentioned the practice of payments received by firms, in return for sending the orders of their unsophisticated customers to a broker for execution. The corollary to that is the payment for order flow on exchanges. There's a bit of a difference, in that most of the markets will pay a rebate to the liquidity provider who is willing to make a price and quote out loud. But it's still payment for order flow. That creates a perverse economic incentive, some people would argue, and it adds complexity. How do we generally feel about that practice? Some people at this conference and elsewhere have advocated for just doing away with that, and the off-exchange payment for order flow, and have even supported that approach on a pilot basis. Does that help us put the genie back in the bottle?

Clark: Our view of maker-taker pricing is that payment for order flow should be on the table.[22] If you think about our market structure, the competing pricing models, and the fragmentation, you'll see that we are pulling natural liquidity providers and natural takers away from each other through these pricing mechanisms. On the one hand, you have the high rebate venues that are attracting all the liquidity providers, providing with us market quality. We would certainly be open to revisiting

[22] For further explanation on this pricing model, see Memorandum. Maker-Taker Fees on Equities Exchanges, SEC Market Structure Advisory Committee. October 20, 2015. https://www.sec.gov/spotlight/emsac/memo-maker-taker-fees-on-equities-exchanges.pdf

access fees and to potentially lowering access fees.[23] But that needs to be done in the context of other possible market reforms. If you simply dropped access fees, you will just get a lot more off-exchange trading activity. The rebate is the substance that is driving the liquidity provider to the exchange. If you don't have a rebate, they're going to go off-exchange to trade, to interact with the segmented flow, so as to queue in front of the displayed liquidity. This can't be addressed in isolation. It has to be addressed with some potential reform measure or tick-size change reform. You also must be careful when you're talking about access fees, when lowering them for the less active securities. That's a part of the market where we're still struggling to get liquidity. It's important to keep it in that area.[24]

Hatheway: One thing that often gets overlooked here is what type of investor provides the quotes. Who puts the orders in displayed markets? If you are a registered market maker – on NASDAQ, or on Direct Edge, or BATS – you have to put up a quote. It doesn't necessarily have to be at the NBBO, but a market maker has to put a quote up. If you are a retail investor, under the order-handling rules of 1997, your orders have to be displayed, if the orders are at the NBBO.[25] To the extent that there are disincentives to quote for market makers or other participants, then setting the NBBO is left to retail investors. We're essentially saying the price will be defined by two groups, the more we do things to disincentive displayed quotes by market makers: One group is retail, because retail orders at the NBBO have to be displayed under the 1997 reforms. The other is institutional algos that choose to display for whatever reason the algo user may have.

Schack: Colin, you talked about tick size. I'd like everyone's thoughts on the idea of a pilot program being discussed now at the SEC, and with people in Congress who would like to see it happen, in order to widen the tick for certain emerging growth, or less liquid securities.[26] There are others who believe that moving to a

---

[23] Ibid.

[24] Market structure reforms were on the table in the following years. For further insight on the issues raised by the speaker, and on the reform momentum, see *The Clock For Market Structure Change Is Ticking. Ivy Schmerken. Wall Street & Technology*. January 7, 2015.

As Schmerken explains in her story: "One of the catalysts for the review was the allegations made by Michael Lewis in *Flash Boys* that the market was "rigged" and that high-frequency traders used latency arbitrage to front-run investor orders on exchanges and dark pools. The media frenzy over the book stirred debate about the complexity and fairness of equity market structure. Some participants feel the market is too complex, distorted by high access fees and payment for order flow."

[25] The SEC's Order Handling Rules of 1997 and Beyond: Perspective and Outcomes of the Landmark Regulation. Richard Lindsey, John Aidan Byrne, and Robert A. Schwartz. *The Journal of Portfolio Management*. Spring 2016 http://www.iijournals.com/doi/pdfplus/10.3905/jpm.2016.42.3.056

[26] The pilot eventually was approved by the Securities and Exchange Commission. See *SEC Approves Pilot Program to Assess Tick Size Impact for Smaller Companies*. Press Release. Securities and Exchange Commission. May 6, 2015. https://www.sec.gov/news/pressrelease/2015-82.html

See also *SEC Approves Pilot Program to Assess Tick Size Impact for Smaller Companies*. Center for Financial Stability, May 7, 2015. http://centerforfinancialstability.org/wp/?p=5987

narrower tick for certain securities would make sense.[27] We have this strange one-size-fits-all approach in the US, which differs from the way things are in other parts of the world.

Clark: We support both. On one end of the spectrum, wider ticks for less active securities make sense. These stocks are very difficult to trade. There are probably 2000 securities that trade less than 250,000 shares a day, and they are very difficult to trade. Once you widen the tick increment, the amount of penny jumping can potentially fall. This encourages more posting of liquidity, and it drives additional trading activity for these names. While we do support it, there is a healthy amount of skepticism as to whether a pilot would work.

On the other end of the spectrum – where there is even stronger evidence to do something – one might support narrowing the tick increments in very active, low-priced securities. I'd say there are about 200 names out there that are trading all day long where people want to trade in narrower increments but can't. They would if you moved to a half-cent increment. We've seen Europe move to tenths of a penny. That could be pretty significant if the US took a similar step in this direction, and it would provide a lot of cost savings to the retail investor.

Hatheway: NASDAQ would certainly support a pilot. But I don't think a tick-size change for displayed quotes alone will achieve very much. The tick is about establishing price priority for executing trades. In a consolidated market, you have clear priority rules. In a highly fragmented market without uniform ticks for trading, despite of Rule 612,[28] you don't really get price priority or any other type of priority. So it'll be interesting to see what happens if the SEC goes ahead with the pilot. But certainly, one-size-fits-all doesn't make any sense.

Schack: Is that one way to get at the internalization problem, as you guys defined it, that if you take half of the vig[29] out of it for the off-exchange guys, they have to, at least, match the quote or provide a tiny bit of price improvement at a half-penny tick rather than one penny? You might see less off-exchange activity as a result?

[27] The idea is that for certain high-volume securities, particularly those with lower share prices, the "natural" spread is actually less than a penny, so those securities are often called "tick constrained." For that reason, market participants sometimes then go to the off-exchange market to do midpoint trades. So, the thinking at the time of the conference was this: If the market is planning to widen the tick for the thinly traded issues, maybe it also would make sense to cut the minimum tick to a half penny for certain high-volume securities with lower share prices. No formal proposals in support of these smaller tick sizes were on the table at the time of the conference. "It was just some market participants talking privately at the conference about this idea," one attendee recalled.

[28] See SEC Division of Market Regulation: Responses to Frequently Asked Questions Concerning Rule 612 (Minimum Pricing Increment) of Regulation NMS https://www.sec.gov/divisions/marketreg/subpenny612faq.htm

[29] "Vig" is a word associated with a charge or interest payments. In this context, the moderator is referring to some kind of restrictions or disincentives on off-exchange trading that would require internalizers to have a live quote in the market or a minimum price improvement.

Clark: Because there is so much liquidity sitting at that one-cent increment, it is probably too much liquidity that is queuing. And there is a significant amount of internalization because a stock wants to trade narrower.

Schack: I have friends on the buy-side who are not too happy that we're at pennies. Can you explain to these folks why going narrower and why the half penny would make sense; why that would be a good thing?[30]

Clark: The bottom line is that these stocks just want to trade narrower, and they should trade narrower. It will result in an immediate reduction of the quoted spread, and that will result in price savings to these institutions. I don't think it overcomplicates things. Europe is at a tenth of a penny. Others are thinking in this way, moving, for example, to a half penny in stocks under $5. It makes sense in terms of the behavior that we are seeing. You are going to see liquidity spread across the half cent and the one cent a little bit more; and this will potentially create more liquidity for the institutions to trade against. It will create more displayed liquidity as well.

Hatheway: I would think you would get smaller ticks anyway, just using the other mechanisms besides the displayed price: taker-maker pricing; exchanges' midpoint orders and more price improvement in dark pools, all have the effect of narrowing the tick for trading. I do think regulation loses, particularly in the long run, when it has to fight economics. In some of these stocks, an optimal tick is not a penny, because a penny is too big, and in some stocks, a penny tick is way too small. When the tick is wrong, we then get into what mechanisms we can all come up with, both for the folks up here who are representing exchanges and the folks out there who are representing broker-dealers and service providers that deal with an unintended consequences of a decision – a decision that was made to simplify how the markets work by creating a uniform penny tick. And it did simplify it in the short run. But, in the long run, everything can and did change.

Clark: A tick increment change goes directly to the retail investor; it goes directly to the institutional customer. Payments of rebates and taker fees drive the order router, and that order router may not be passing those savings on to the end investor.

Schack: In most cases they aren't. We talked a lot about the impact of modern market structure fragmentation on market quality. One of the other big by-products of this is system integrity. We've had a lot of events of this nature happen in the past few years. Go back to the Flash Crash,[31] the BATS and Facebook

---

[30] See footnote 28 for further guidance.

[31] The Flash Crash of May 6, 2010, lasted about 36 min, erasing 998.5 points in the Dow Jones Industrial Average and then quickly recouped much of the losses as the various indexes rapidly rebounded in these high-speed, electronic trading phenomena.

IPOs,[32] and the Knight situation on August of 2011.[33] More recently, we had a major outage with the Securities Information Processor, or SIP, which is the consolidated tape for NASDAQ-listed stocks.[34] Since many people don't have a full grasp on what exactly happened with that SIP outage, Colin, can you spend a minute taking us through that?

Clark: The good news is that the SIP has a good track record for system uptime and for system availability. The bad news is that we have had a string of three events in a short period of time which highlighted the vulnerability of the SIP. Thursday, August 22, 2013, was probably the biggest issue when the NASDAQ SIP had software and fail-over issues that led to a market closure of 3 h.[35] There was another issue on Wednesday, September 4th. It was a NASDAQ SIP hardware issue that brought the market down.[36] There was yet another one on Monday, September 16th that was in the options market.[37] The options SIP had a software change issue which led to that market dropping or halting for 30 min. The good news is that these particular issues have been addressed. The participants and the SIPs are moving forward to develop an action plan to strengthen the SIPs' resiliency. That includes exploring potential SIP backup options if one of the SIPs goes down.

Schack: Bob has urged me to give the floor to the audience for questions.

---

[32] This BATS IPO referenced here was scrapped after a software glitch sent its shares plunging a fraction of a cent within seconds when the IPO was attempted on March 23, 2012. On April 14 2016, Bats Global Markets ultimately priced its long-awaited initial public offering at $19.

See *Facebook IPO: What the %$#! happened*? Julianne Pepitone, *CNNMoney*, May 23, 2012, http://money.cnn.com/2012/05/23/technology/facebook-ipo-what-went-wrong/index htm

[33] *Aug. 1 stock trading fiasco costs Knight $604 M*, *USA Today*, October 17, 2012. According to the opening paragraph in this AP story: "The Knight Capital Group trading firm said it lost $764.3 million in the third quarter because of a software glitch that flooded the stock market with trades one day in August, causing dozens of stocks to fluctuate wildly." http://www.usatoday.com/story/money/markets/2012/10/17/knight-capital-earnings/1638817/

[34] "The Security Information Processor (SIP) links the US markets by processing and consolidating all protected bid/ask quotes and trades from every trading venue into a single, easily consumed data feed." Source: Consolidated Tape Association.

More broadly, the NYSE and NASDAQ, at time of writing, each operated a SIP for US stock exchanges, the former showing the best bid and offer for NYSE-listed stocks, the latter showing the NBBO for NASDAQ stocks. These data processors consolidate quote and trade data for stocks listed on their exchanges. The data is then disseminated for a fee to investors, market data providers, and others. NYSE also operated a SIP for options exchanges.

[35] See *Shutdown at Nasdaq Is Traced to Software. Michael De La Merced, New York Times. August 29, 2013 http://dealbook.nytimes.com/2013/08/29/nasdaq-blames-a-surge-of-data-for-trading-halt/?_r=0*

[36] *Glitch hits Nasdaq system at center of trading outage*, John McCrank, *Reuters*. September 4, 2013 http://www.reuters.com/article/us nasdaq-outage-idUSBRE9830Y920130905

[37] *Tech snafu halts options trading*. Mark DeCambre. *New York Post*. September 16, 2013. http://nypost.com/2013/09/16/tech-snafu-halts-options-trading/

Steven Sacks [Chief Compliance Officer, FBN Securities]: NASDAQ is the processor of the SIP, and the last report from the association in the second quarter of 2013 noted how high-frequency trading participants still had access to direct feeds when the SIP was not working properly. In fact, Bob Griefeld, on August 23 on CNBC, stated how "We knew professional traders had access to individual data feeds, but the traditional long investor, retail investors now didn't have the same information. Because of that we halted the market. The high-frequency firms would have access to proprietary feeds from individual exchanges. The consolidated feed, which we operate, had a problem, wasn't giving quotes out. We had to halt the market because of that. We didn't want to have a situation where information is asymmetry, as you say.[38]" So, these are the facts. And the simple question I have is, do we have a two-tier market for data, and is that fair?

Hatheway: Everybody's a broker, and everybody has access to high speed stuff![39] No doubt, you've heard that explanation before. Well, most people do not have the technology to take advantage of it, at least on an individual level. The brokers all certainly do. There are multiple ways to get data. Can you call it two-tier? Well, you just have, but I wouldn't. It's just different types of data products that cater to different needs. Investors need the NBBO and little more, and the SIP rolls up the NBBO for them.

A trader doesn't necessarily need the NBBO. Many of the trading engines sitting within our data center are only going to trade NASDAQ, and are not paying too much attention to what is going on in other worlds. They are just trying to match supply and demand on NASDAQ. We offer data that is tailored to different participant needs. There is nothing that we can do to get information to you as fast as someone who is co-located with NASDAQ.[40]

You and I have been in this business a few years. You probably remember that NASDAQ used to delay data to members in New York, so that members in San Francisco had time to respond. In the Nordics, OMX used to randomize data, so that Copenhagen would have a chance to respond to a data center in Stockholm. We can do that, the technology is there, and it is quite old. The trouble is that everybody has to have delayed data and only delayed data, otherwise you're left with one person having an informational advantage. If, for a matter of public policy, the industry and regulators want to delay a message, if we want to randomize again and, if we want to eliminate any kind of speed advantage that way, we could do it.

---

[38] "Asymmetric information, sometimes referred to as information failure, is present whenever one party to an economic transaction possesses greater material knowledge than the other party." Source: Investopedia.

[39] Clearly, the speaker was speaking in jest, to make his point.

[40] This refers to the ability of market participants to gain advantages in the speed of their trade executions and price quote data through advanced technology, specifically the "co-location" of their computer servers near stock exchanges' computers. That lowers the so-called latency, a critical factor in high-speed trade executions. The practice is regarded as legal though it has many critics.

Your point, in my mind, is fundamentally about this. I've got some alpha, I want to keep it, I don't want to worry about who is getting ahead of me because they are faster. If it creates (for us) an image problem, an integrity problem more on the reputational side, then that is something that we need to deal with. Right now, today's markets seem like an efficient, relatively low-cost way to run the market. The markets let people, when their order is actually in the hand of a trading engine, trade as well as the order possibly could. But there are other market models, and we operate other models outside the US. Colin, you guys may have operated different structure in the various geographies where you operate as well. Operating different models creates other problems, the main one being that it is not globally efficient.

Clark: Everyone gets the proprietary feed, everyone has access to the proprietary feeds, and they get it at the same time. Everyone has access to the SIP feeds, and they get it at the same time. But it takes the SIP more time to process the data because they are aggregating the proprietary feeds; they're calculating the NBBO and so on. The key is to – and you hit on it – it is to minimize the amount of processing time in the SIP. You indicated that NASDAQ's SIP has come down dramatically, but it is still too slow.

Justin Schack: Gentlemen, thank you very much.

Chapter 2
A Global Perspective

Huseyin Erkan

Bob Schwartz: Huseyin Erkan and I have been well acquainted, both professionally and personally, for many wonderful and productive years. When we first met each other we were really young guys, and one of us is still young. Guess who? [laughter]. Huseyin was here, participating in this same Baruch conference series, 2 years ago. I asked him back today to speak on his own as our guest. I like his interesting thoughts; I like his ideas; and so I extend a big warm welcome to Huseyin.

Huseyin Erkan: I am wearing a different hat this year. I'm now the CEO of the World Federation of Exchanges (WFE). Before that I was the Chairman and CEO of the Istanbul Stock Exchange. The Istanbul Stock Exchange is a mid-sized exchange, based in a city that is partly in Europe, and partly in Asia.[1]

I will present a little refresher course, giving you a world-wide perspective of developments outside the United States. The rest of the world is facing different types of issues and problems than the US. Some of the problems here in the US are too sophisticated for the rest of the world to handle, and they may not even exist for years to come in some non-US countries. Why? Because of the impact of regulation in the US.

Let me explain. Regulation shapes our markets. Markets depend on how you regulate them, on how you define the institutions operating in their respective countries. Regulation determines the ultimate shape of the capital markets. Do markets really change that much from one country to another? Maybe not that much in the area of regulation, but certainly they change in the areas of practice and enforcement.

[1] See, website: http://borsaistanbul.com/en/

H. Erkan (✉)
World Federation of Exchanges, London, UK

© Springer Nature Switzerland AG 2019

R. A. Schwartz et al. (eds.), *Market Integrity*, Zicklin School of Business Financial Markets Series, https://doi.org/10.1007/978-3-030-02871-8_2

We talk about fragmentation in the US and in the European Union. That word does not apply to markets elsewhere in the world, because the exchanges in these parts are still regarded as utilities, even if they are private (and most are not). They are still the central utilities that gather orders from market participants to discover a price that will set the value of a company and, in turn, will attract both investors and issuers to the market. Basic stuff, yes, but that is how it shakes out. Exchanges still play a very big role in the economic development of a country.

Market integrity is a very broad term. It starts with investor education. Maybe it's not news to you in the US, but it's still a problem in many other countries. Less than 2% of the worldwide population is directly involved in the capital markets, or have any investments in capital market instruments in many countries around the world. The order processing, intermediation, matching engines, and the price discovery mechanism that belong to the exchange infrastructure, and also the price discovery of an asset, are all essential parts of market integrity. Is anybody abusing the markets? That is the surveillance side of market integrity, and it is tied together with the appropriate regulation and enforcement.

We've had regulations, Reg NMS[2] and MiFID,[3] for example, that have created problems. These led to the proverbial unintended consequences. Yet regulators around the globe never want to hurt the markets because they are acting on behalf of their governments, or on behalf of the investors and their rights. The intention is not to disturb the markets. The intention is to make the markets more efficient. Nevertheless, regulation sometimes ends up distorting the markets as we have seen in some countries, such as the US and EU, where it has led to the aforementioned market fragmentation.

I'll present some slides and then talk about the World Federation of Exchanges, including our mission; what we're really trying to protect, or defend, on behalf of exchanges worldwide.

Exhibit 2.1 shows the trends in the global markets. We've seen the overall value of an exchange's order book share of trading declining since the crisis, from pre-crisis 2007 and throughout the crisis. What you see here is really on-exchange trading. It is on-exchange trading that is in decline. Last year, 2013, there were some signs it was moving back up a bit. The US and the European exchange operators have been affected severely throughout the financial crisis. However, it's not really the financial crisis that is the root cause of this. It coincides with market fragmentation in Europe – resulting in a mess in Europe – and all these market structure changes in the US. You can see that the on-exchange trading volumes are sliding in

[2] Reg NMS (Regulation National Market System) was adopted by the Securities and Exchange Commission in 2005 and, 2 years later, introduced to further advance the ideals of a national market system. The regulation includes the order protection, or trade-through rule; access rule (fair access) to market data including quotations; rules on sub-penny trading and on market data.

[3] Markets in Financial Instruments Directive I, or MiFID I, introduced in October 2010, was followed by the second MiFID proposals, or MiFID II, in September 2012, both aiming for the reform and harmonization of European area markets. MiFID II shifts the European regulatory regime from a principles-based to a more US-style, rules-based regulatory model.

the US, Europe, the Middle East and Africa (EMEA). Apart from Europe, the markets in the Middle East and Africa really don't count for much in terms of volume. In other parts of the world, there is hardly any fragmentation. They are not affected by fragmentation. You can see that they are pretty stable, that they are at the same level they started out at prior to the crisis. In Latin America, Brazil takes the largest share, and its on-exchange trading is booming.

Exhibit 2.1

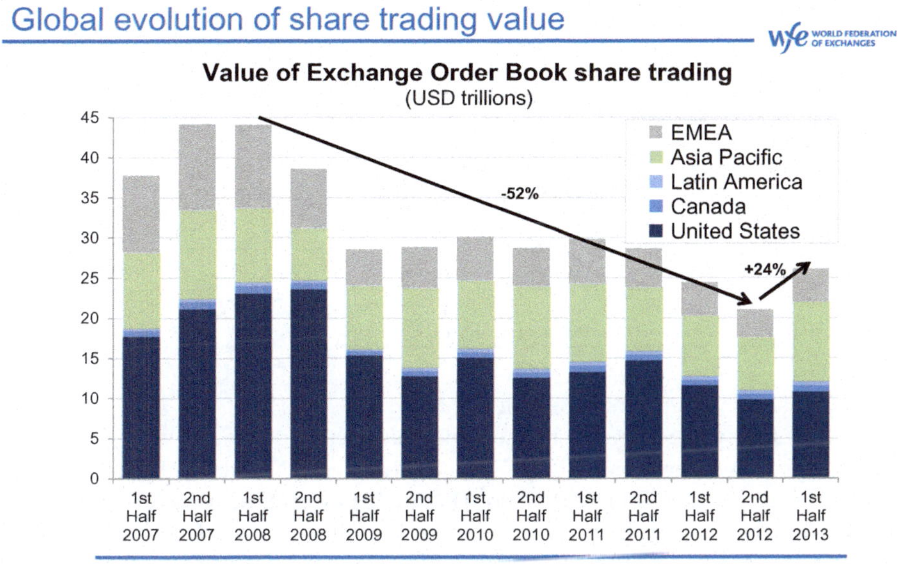

Exhibit 2.2 is highlighting the American and European markets. When we talk about fragmentation, we're really talking about the US, Canada and Europe; the non-fragmented being the markets in South America, Asia, Pacific, the Middle East and Africa. The value of exchange order book share trading in the US and EU has decreased, resulting in a decline in the total share in the markets. By contrast, in the non-fragmented markets, the major exchanges have the majority of the market shares.

Exhibit 2.2

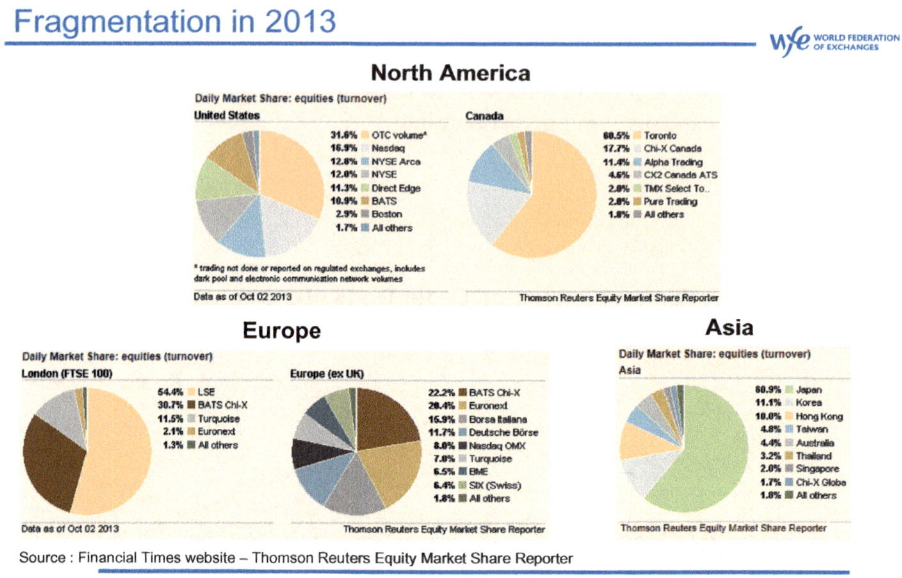

So, what else has been happening?

The average value of on-exchange trades has been in decline as well. And where has it been going down? Mostly in Europe. The average value of orders in Europe has declined from $30,000 to $11,700. That's a big drop, almost one third of what it used to be. By contrast, in the US, the average trading value of a contract is similar to what it used to be in 2008. The decline has been much more dramatic in Europe.

The equities and interest rate derivative market figures are all from our own database. The exchanges that are members of the WFE report their figures every month. We try to collate them and publish some related reports. So we see for the interest rate and the index-based equity derivatives, as well as the ETFs versus the single stocks, that there's been little change. But I think the change in the trading of index-based derivatives is really due to the increase in the contract size of the KOSPI index derivative, which is the most actively traded index-based equity contract in the world.[4] It has really affected its total trading negatively and, therefore, the total trading in the rest of the world. It is now stabilizing. Exchange-traded interest rate derivatives came down a little during the crisis, but now we are back to pre-crisis levels. These are all on exchange trading figures.

What is happening to the IPO market? IPOs went down in numbers during the crisis, but now they are moving back up. The total value of funds raised was affected very badly right after the crisis. We have seen a comeback in 2010 and 2011. But in 2012, and I think even in 2013, we see a bit of a tapering off due to a slowdown in the Asian markets, especially in China. The IPOs are not as high in value as they

[4] KOSPI, or the Korea *Composite Stock Price Index, is the index of all* common stocks *traded on the stock market of the* Korea Exchange.

once were. The Chinese used to bring a lot of companies into the market. Right now they have slowed down and, in fact, a lot of the Chinese companies are going abroad to list.

When we talk about market structure [Exhibit 2.3], and the trade repositories, or the trade reporting facilities (TRFs), we see the share of the trading volumes reported to TRFs has increased in the last 5 years, from 15% of total trading, to over 35% of total trading.[5] In the US equity markets, off-exchange market share has been growing over the years. The increase is represented on the slide with the 10-day moving average indicator. It's getting close to three times as big as it once was. The number of securities, with over 40% of TRF market share, has almost doubled, to about 3855 companies, from around 2000 companies just over the past 2 years.

Exhibit 2.3

Increasing share of off-exchange trades

WFE WORLD FEDERATION OF EXCHANGES

- TRF-share of trading has increased in the last five years, from 15% of total trading to over 35%.
- Since September 2012, TRF levels have exceeded 35% on 64 (out of 140) days.
- Number of Securities: The number of securities with >40% "TRF" share has more than doubled in the past year to over 49% of total stocks.

In Exhibit 2.3, we see the impact on price efficiency. The off-exchange trading facilities are not subject to the same regulatory requirements as the regulated exchanges, and there's discriminatory access. It's all discretionary. There is no pre-trade transparency and limited post-trade transparency. There is the ability to trade at the NBBO[6] without quoting and the ability to offer the minimum sub-penny price improvements, which is totally different from the regulated exchanges. Introduction of a tick size programme has been discussed for a very long time in the US. It still

[5] In the United States, Trade Reporting Facilities, or TRF's, are venues for Alternative Trading Systems, or ATSs, to report trades to the consolidated tape.

[6] In simple terms, the National Best Bid and Offer, NBBO, requires brokers under US regulation, to guarantee that customers receive the best prevailing ask price when they buy securities, and the best prevailing bid price when they sell.

has not come to a conclusion.[7] As for on-exchange and regulated markets, you need to think about the pluses and minuses, the advantages and disadvantages, as well as confirmation procedures with the regulators. By contrast, in the unregulated trading venues you can do anything you like. There is no regulation stopping you from offering different price levels, or different tick levels. The spreads are wider for securities with more than 40% of the TRF share. This is consolidated average daily volume. Yes, more and more trades are moving away from the regulated exchanges. But what is that really accomplishing? The spreads are growing as well. Is that really efficient? No, we don't see the efficiency.

Much of the activity lacks price improvement. Lit market, mid-point orders offer substantial price improvement, of course.[8] Personally, I think the mid-price is an innovative way of matching orders. But I don't think it is really a direct part of price discovery. It is a no-brainer. Exchanges never offered it before; now they can do it through different means. Intermediaries who are internalizing have been doing it for years and years. It does not add up to price discovery. Because it takes away the orders that are supposed to be collected by the regulated exchanges to discover a price efficiently. Mid-point orders, on the other hand, offer an opportunity for the orders to be away from the exchanges and central order books. The spreads then get wider and the mid-points get even more attractive as a result. It is a self-fulfilling prophecy. I do not call that a market.

Here are some examples of effective regulation in Exhibit 2.4: In Australia, the fines and regulations have been very effective. ASIC, the regulatory authority in Australia,[9] has regulated the markets in such a way that the cost-recovery regime coincided with a sharp step-down in the order-to-trade ratios.[10] In Australia, any trade that goes to the dark, or the non-exchange environment should, similar to Canada, show that there is a price improvement. In the months since it has been in place, the trade-to-order ratio has declined. In fact, the Australian Stock Exchange trade-to-order ratio has been quiet stable. Indeed, Chi-Ex,[11] when it entered the Australian market as an MTF,[12] started getting a lot of market share. But the order-to-trade ratio was huge. This new regulation has brought it down. The order-to-trade

---

[7] As of writing, a tick-size pilot program in the US was scheduled to take effect in October 2016, the goal being to stimulate more trading in small companies via wider trading increments. US exchanges started quoting stocks in pennies in 2001, ending the practice for over 200 years of pricing equities in fractions.

[8] A lit market refers to venues that display the various bids and offers in stocks. By contrast, dark markets, or Dark Pools, do not display prices.

[9] Australia Securities & Investments Commission (ASIC). http://asic.gov.au/

[10] The order to trade ratio is the ratio of orders sent to the trading venue(s) compared to the number of those same orders matched or transacted. Therefore, the higher the ratio, the less efficient is the trading venue.

[11] See, *Chi-X launch – what does it mean for the Australian market? The Conversation. Carole Comerton-Forde, October 31, 2011.* http://theconversation.com/chi-x-launch-what-does-it-mean-for-the-australian-market-3900

[12] A regulatory term for a non-exchange trading venue known as a multilateral trading facility.

ratio has declined on Chi-Ex. But as an MTF which offers some flexibility, Chi-Ex's market share has been increasing since it was introduced. So, yes, it has helped lower the order-to-trade ratios, but it has also helped increase competition.

Exhibit 2.4

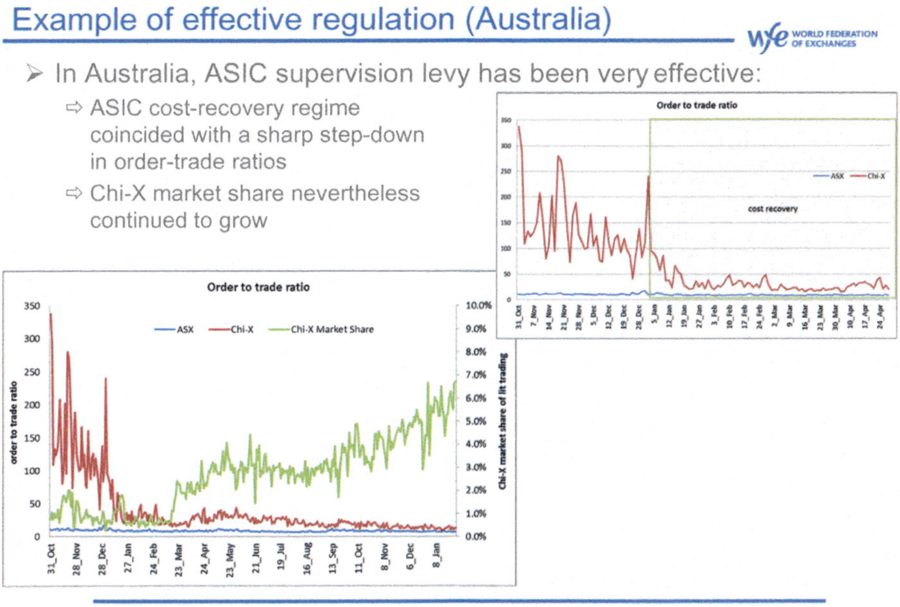

In summary, competition has not been impacted by this in Australia. Chi-Ex share in the market has been growing, but its order-to-trade ratio has dropped tremendously. This is an example of an effective regulation in action. A similar thing is happening in Canada [Exhibit 2.5]. I think we are seeing similar results. The rule in Canada is the same as in Australia in that any trade routed to the dark venues has to show a price improvement. Average quarted spreads fell by 25% in Canada compared with the 10 most active stocks in the US where the same regulation does not exist. These 10 most active stocks have actually increased by 21%.This is another example of effective regulation helping to bring the order-to-trade ratio down, which in turn has helped quoted spreads go down. And we, at the WFE, applaud the Canadian and Australian regulators.

Exhibit 2.5

Example of effective regulation (Canada)

WORLD FEDERATION OF EXCHANGES

- Canadian rule on dark liquidity in October 2012: Meaningful price improvement (generally 1c) or size threshold (50 round lots or C$100K) requirements to internalize.
- Average **quoted spread** fell by 25% and increased by 20.9% for US 10 most active stocks.
- Average **intraday volatility** fell by 17% increased by 16.85% for 10 most active US stocks.

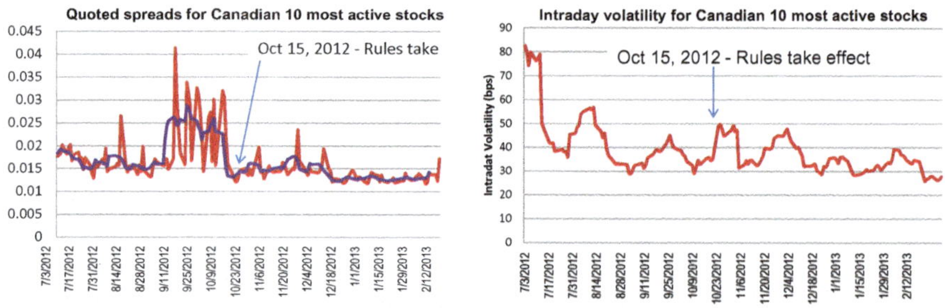

Source: Bloomberg

I will not delve into algorithmic trading much, nor into any of the high-frequency trading (HFT). But I will just say one or two things about the HFT as a principal. Unfortunately, in the news as well as amongst the regulators, HFT is seen as an evil, as a tool to abuse markets, or as a tool to provide some means of getting ahead of the market. Some regulators tend to be very skeptical about HFT as well. Regardless, we have seen that HFT has tapered off, as can be seen in Exhibit 2.6, in the past 18 months. When the share of HFT to total trades comes to a certain level, the expected advantage is no longer there. However, the exchanges are coming back with measures to follow HFT. HFT is an order processing tool. It is the result of technology. HFT is not, by itself, a tool for people to abuse the markets. Market abuse is regulated as an offense, and supervised by the regulators and the exchanges. Abusive behavior can happen manually too. We think that HFT actually provides a lot of liquidity to the markets, and it helps price discovery as a result.

Exhibit 2.6

High Frequency Trading

WORLD FEDERATION OF EXCHANGES

- HFT has become global: Around 50% of cash equity volumes in US and 40% in Europe
- Mature market: Volumes and profitability are now trending downward

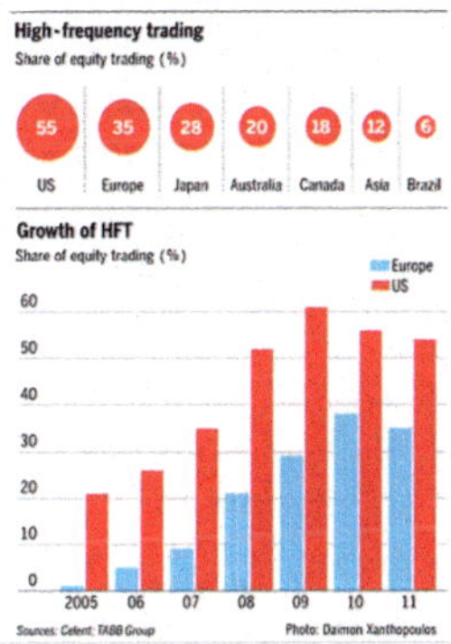

Source: *Lobby plan brings proprietary trading out of shadows*, Financial Times, June 5, 2012

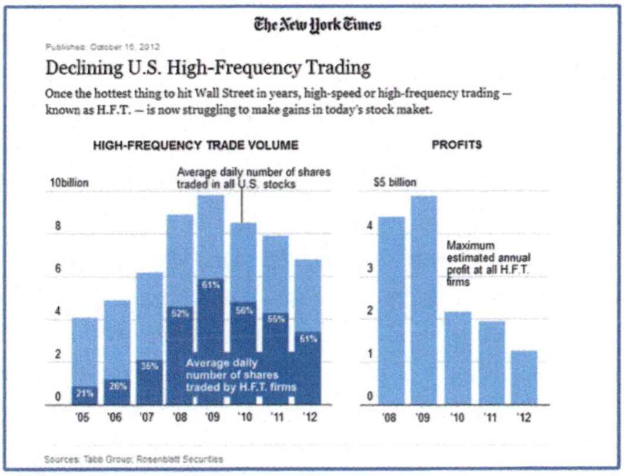

The exchanges need to follow what HFT does, or how it can be used in their markets to avoid abuse and any unfair advantage. At the end of the day, the regulators look at market integrity with the perspective of protecting investor rights. This means they look to see if there is any abusive behavior that uses tools to get ahead of other market participants; or are affecting market efficiency negatively. And this means that exchanges have to increase their surveillance; they have to work together with the regulators and the other exchanges to accomplish this. How about the multilateral trading facilities? Sorry, they don't do that. They have no obligation. Exchanges work together with the regulators, and must have measures to surveil the markets in an efficient way. The other trading venues don't have that obligation.

The exchanges have the oversight of the data for the volumes; they look at the order-to-trade ratios; they have specific fee incentives to control volumes; they have enhanced surveillance tools; they may have circuit breakers; kill-switches; oversight of algos, and all sorts of other methodologies to keep market integrity intact. They work together with the regulators to provide this integrity.

There are some challenges in information technology, or IT. We have seen problems occurring here and there with glitches and technology issues. Still, technology is here to stay, it is growing and developing very, very fast. The problem is the disconnect between the regulation and the marketplace. We think there should be much closer cooperation between the marketplace and regulators.

Cybercrime work we have conducted with IOSCO[13] has produced illuminating results. In a study of WFE member exchanges, slightly more than half (52%) last year experienced a cyberattack; 90% view cybercrime as a potential systemic risk.

[13] International Organization of Securities Commissions. http://www.iosco.org/

And senior management of these exchanges is totally aware of it. Indeed, they take measures to mitigate any kind of risk associated with cybercrime, or the abuse of technology itself. At the WFE, we believe that technology as an issue should be studied very closely, together with the market practitioners. New technology should be well tested before it is introduced to the market.

The marketplace, especially in the US and Europe, has become extremely complicated. Nowadays, when you have an update in the technology of a US exchange, it affects other exchanges because a US exchange must be compatible with the NBBO requirements of Reg NMS. This provides an opportunity to see what is available in all the venues, and to route the orders accordingly. That means that everyone, ideally, should be interoperable. That's good, it sounds nice, but technically it is so difficult. Technology needs to develop, and it needs to do so with the supervision of the regulators.

The regulators have to understand the complexities of the technology as well. Now, this coupling amongst the market participants is a very important issue. I ran an exchange. I know the complications involved in running an exchange, and in providing access to market participants, being the single exchange operator in a country. You're talking about a plethora of exchanges in the US, in addition to more exchanges across the EU; and then there are an array of MTFs, as well as all sorts of other trading venues that actually see and route orders to each other. Technology has to play a vital role. Let's say you have all these compatible access tools for technology. In reality, with the increase in transactions turnaround and speeds, it is not easy to maintain your own technology and still stay competitive. It takes time and, as a previous panelist said, it will cost a lot of money. This cost will be met by the investors, the exchanges, and the intermediaries. But if it is for a positive objective, it should be supported. Technology is something you cannot hold back. It will help markets develop and become more efficient.

The WFE supports competition. We believe that the regulators must promote market structures that foster order transmission in a free, transparent, fair, and competitive environment. Unfortunately, in recent years, regulations intended to promote competition between the exchanges have been misused to enable the growth of venues designed to avoid competition.

The WFE is concerned about the integrity and efficiency of fragmented, complex, and dark markets, particularly as it relates to price formation, surveillance, and market resiliency. Market participants are increasingly discouraged from posting competing prices in lit venues. And the evidence indicates that the spreads are wider than they could otherwise be. Similarly, diminishing transparency and unfair access lead to market complexity, and make markets less capable of handling volatility. Finally, the WFE is concerned that a greater share of equity trading occurs away from the full regulatory protection offered by the regulated exchanges.

The WFE is a trade association that aims to be the advocate for the exchange sector. We are prepared to work closely with the regulators, especially IOSCO, on many issues. We hope that we will be able to help the regulators introduce better, more efficient, and more useful regulation. More regulation does not necessarily mean better regulation. But I certainly think that useful and intelligent regulation is required in our markets.

I thank you again Bob for inviting me. Questions?

Nori Jyote: [Bear Lab Technology and Baruch College adjunct]: Why are these things happening as you describe them? What has technology done in this regard? Being a human being is more important than harnessing only technology. Both have to go together.

Erkan: That's a very complex question. I can say that market integrity involves investor education and financial education. That is the crux of the whole problem. If you don't have it, then everyone will look at a market as a gambling casino. Unfortunately, that is not how it is. Sometime people buy and sell things without knowing what they are buying and selling. Everyone should pay more attention to investor education.

Jim Ross: Does the WFE have any MTF or Alternative Trading System[14] members? If not, why not? And if so, why?

Erkan: No, we don't. The WFE stands for the regulated exchanges. It's the World Federation of Exchanges. And the WFE has a few criteria for membership. As long as a trading venue is recognized as a regulated exchange by the respective country's regulator, it becomes a potential candidate for membership. Without being a regulated exchange, our statues do not allow that.

Ross: Just a follow up. Alternative Trading Systems, or ATSs, are regulated.

Erkan: Not as exchanges.

Ross: If they did a certain amount of volume, they would become qualified as exchanges. Don't you think it would be useful to engage that conversation with ATSs and MTFs, to incorporate these new environments into your organization?

Erkan: I agree, and once in a while we do talk to them. The more they are regulated and become more a part of the regulated trading environment, with the same obligations, with the same rules, with the same principals, I think we will be more ready to accept them. Rather than accepting them into our membership, our next move may be to involve them in the same discussion groups. We may even look at some of their data. WFE is a major source of exchange data. But then, as I showed, exchanges in some countries are only accounting for 30–35% of the market share. The rest of it is over-the-counter, or OTC, or in non-exchange venues. We must be able to capture more than that. Our sister organization in Europe FESE[15] has started reporting MTF figures as part of their data.

We will end with that thought. Thank you.

---

[14] Alternative Trading System (ATS) is the US regulatory term for a non-exchange trading venue that matches buyers and sellers in transactions. ATSs include ECNs, Dark Pools and call markets.

[15] Federation of European Securities Exchanges. http://www.fese.eu/

Chapter 3
Integrity of Price Discovery: Perspective of Customers

Ian Domowitz, John Donahue, William Lishman, Timothy J. Mahoney, Lin Peng, and Adam Sussman

Bob Schwartz: I want to underline a special fact about our moderator, Ian Domowitz: We are friends from way back. Our friendship started when Ian was an academician. And Ian hasn't changed that much. He may look spiffier, but he really hasn't changed that much. Please welcome Ian.

Ian Domowitz: It is one of the hidden costs of moving to Wall Street. You have to give up your jeans and flannel shirts and actually put on a suit. It does happen. The discussion so far has been very interesting. Thank you, Bob, for inviting us all.

Moderators have a hard mission. Our job, in principle, is to keep things moving along. I have watched many moderators trying to start a panel. Some of them, like Justin Schack, a previous moderator this morning, say, "Hey, let's go." There are others who spend a lot of time on opening remarks, or they make a speech. For myself, I don't like going first because you can't just make up some of the stuff you hear as you sit through a conference.

I. Domowitz (✉)
ITG Solutions Network, Inc., New York, NY, USA

ITG, Inc., New York, NY, USA

J. Donahue
Fidelity Capital Markets, Boston, MA, USA

W. Lishman
Schroders, London, UK

T. J. Mahoney
BIDS Trading, LP, New York, NY, USA

L. Peng
Zicklin School of Business, Baruch College CUNY, New York, NY, USA

A. Sussman
TABB Group, Westborough, MA, USA

© Springer Nature Switzerland AG 2019

R. A. Schwartz et al. (eds.), *Market Integrity*, Zicklin School of Business Financial Markets Series, https://doi.org/10.1007/978-3-030-02871-8_3

That said, I'd like to start off by getting into the notion of price discovery in various ways. For example, Bob Schwartz gave a very interesting talk this morning about the nature of price discovery, and he made a very thoughtful comment that I couldn't quite get my head around.[1] That is, that an individual price would have integrity. Now, I was taught that price discovery is a process; it's the revelation of information through trading, which means that there is no single price that has integrity in some sense. As a matter of fact, the one place I saw Bob pause was where, in a continuous market – which is really what markets are these days, for the most part – there is no such thing as equilibrium. No one has been able to figure one out. So there is no such thing as an equilibrium price, and it becomes very hard to talk about the integrity of any given price during the trading day.

I loved the stuff earlier today about the aliens! That really resonated because my pre-equities experience was all in derivatives.[2] I once felt a little like that too, an alien, but here's what I would point out, notwithstanding Frank Hatheway's remarks about 18 years of data being a lot of data.[3] If that alien had been dropped on the face of the earth around the turn of the century, I mean the 1900s, that alien would have seen a hundred different exchanges. Not 13 or 18 or however many we count. That's only in the US. And there was no connectivity back then at all. The issue of fragmentation is a little slippery given its effect on markets and the way we talk about it.

There was also talk today of high-frequency trading. Essentially, you heard two views at this conference. You heard the exchange view which, fundamentally speaking, is to regulate behavior, which I agree with. And you have heard another view that says, no, this is an evil thing. I would point out that back in 1962, accounting for the size of the market back then and today, there was a flash crash much more violent than what we observed in May 2010.[4] Back in the old days, high-frequency trading meant you were on the floor, and dark pools meant you had cards in your pocket, and co-location[5] meant you had an office next to the exchange. We saw exactly that same behavior we attribute to these new players and new competitions.

---

[1] Preface: Opening Remarks. The Low Down on High Intraday Volatility: Robert Schwartz, Speiser Professor of Finance, Zicklin School of Business, Baruch College, CUNY.

[2] In his varied and distinguished career as an academic and on Wall Street, the moderator was also a consultant to the US Commodity Futures Trading Commission (CFTC), the regulator for the US derivatives markets, with its central regional office in Chicago.

[3] See Chap. 1: *Integrity of Price Discovery: Perspectives of Exchanges.*

[4] See The Intelligent Investor. *Back to the Future: Lessons From the Forgotten 'Flash Crash' of 1962.* Jason Zweig, *Wall Street Journal*, May 29, 2010. http://www.wsj.com/articles/SB10001424052748703957604575272791511469272. The story quoted the opening of a story from the Wall Street Journal of May 29, 1962: "The stock market careened downward yesterday, leaving traders shaken and exhausted. The Dow Jones Industrial Average fell 5.7% that day, down 34.95, the second-largest point decline then on record."

[5] This refers to the ability of market participants to gain advantages in the speed of their trade executions and price-quote data through advanced technology, specifically the "co-location" of their computer servers near stock exchanges' computers. That lowers so-called latency, a critical factor in high-speed trade executions. The practice is regarded as legal though it has many critics.

Then I listened to the exchange panel. That was remarkable. I apologize to the members of that panel for missing the last 10 min. During the first 50 min, the speakers on that panel said something about price discovery and the integrity of price discovery. Those two words were not even mentioned at any time during the presentation I heard. That says more about conferences, perhaps, than about substance. It also suggests that the notion of price discovery is something we skirt around.

And the off-exchange trading? Oh, I love these statistics because they are nonattributable to exactly what off-exchange means. I would also point out that a little bit of history would be good here. That is because, in the late 1990s and the early 2000s, when I was much more active in the study of electronic markets, over 50% of the volume in Europe, which was totally electronic in that period, was done off exchange. Over 50%! Those are published statistics and very, very well known. We are crying here in the US that we are now edging up to 38%, as though this is somehow a crisis.[6] I'm not so sure. I think a sense of history is a good guide.

One of the panelists pointed out to me that the term, price discovery, may be generic, perhaps even a little bit dated. We have been talking about it from the beginning, especially the beginnings of the electronic exchange revolution. One panelist noted to me, prior to this session, that the only folks talking about price discovery are exchanges and academics. I'll say the exchanges just didn't talk about it. And there was a recent speech by SEC Chairwoman, Mary Jo White, that I found much evolved in its thinking in many ways.[7] But I was also curious, as I read it, if price discovery was at all mentioned, let alone introduced as a theme. It's actually only mentioned once. It says, "A strong secondary market generates price discovery that helps efficiently allocate capital." That was it.

Somehow we all take this for granted. But it's all about price discovery. We don't observe any fundamental value at any given point in time. We mistake price discovery with the notion of correctly priced liquidity. Having said that, I want to start with the basics. I want to ask Lin, who's here from the Baruch faculty, to give us a definition from her perspective.

Lin Peng: I agree with what you said. Price discovery is an elusive concept. I don't think that there is a great unified measure of price discovery. In Bob Schwartz's earlier talk this morning, he looks at intraday volatility accentuation as an indication of inefficient price discovery. In previous academic studies, people have used other measures. Some of them are related to liquidity measures, such as spread or price impact, and so on and so forth. In the recent project that I am working on with Bob and my colleagues Jian Hua and Sila Alan, we are looking at a new measure of price discovery.[8] In particular, we are looking at the quality of the price at 10 o'clock in the morning [EST].

---

[6] Referring to off-exchange trading in the USA.

[7] *Focusing on Fundamentals: The Path to Address Equity Market Structure*. SEC Chairwoman, Mary Jo White. Security Traders Association 80th Annual Market Structure Conference, Washington, D.C. Oct. 2, 2013 https://www.sec.gov/News/Speech/Detail/Speech/1370539857459

[8] Hua, Peng, Schwartz and Alan (2016). *"Are Stocks Priced to Yield a Non-Resiliency Premium?"*

Why are we interested in the price quality at 10 o'clock? We believe that the opening half an hour of the trading day is a critical period when a lot of price discoveries occur. Therefore, looking at the quality of prices at 10 o'clock will give us a fair indication of the degree and efficiency of price discovery.

I can talk about how we assess the quality of prices at 10 o'clock. We are looking at intraday return patterns. For example, say if price is efficiently discovered at 10 o'clock, and if you have a stock at the open at $50, and at 10 o'clock something happened, like exogenous news, and the price shoots up to $55. If that's a well-discovered price, then that should be an unbiased predictor of the closing price. However, if it happens that the price starts at $50 at 10 o'clock, jumps to $55, and then, at the end of the day, drops back to $52, that means the price at 10 o'clock is actually overshot. So, the 10 o'clock price is not an efficient price.

Basically, we are looking at the correlation of the opening half an hour return, with the remainder of the day return. A negative, intraday return autocorrelation indicates that price discovery is inefficient. That's our new measure of price discovery. We are going to investigate how investors evaluate different stocks with different degrees of price discovery efficiencies and how, accordingly, they price these stocks.

Domowitz: In the context of Bob Schwartz's earlier discussion, I will point out that unbiased does not mean *not* volatile. A statistic can be extremely volatile and still be unbiased. I must tell you that this panel is completely unrehearsed, that I refused to have a preconference conference call (although I did make contact with a couple of people). I'd like to ask William Lishman to talk about something that he raised to me. That is, we talked about a market system, an order book with real volume. But it seems as though the integrity of price discovery, if we can sort of pin that down (at least in the abstract), should depend on the size of the trade and even on the investment objective. I wonder if you can speak on that a little bit – I found that intriguing.

William Lishman: When I first saw the topic of this panel – and it's an enormous topic, being global in scope, you could take it in many different ways – I decided to focus on the US. The market has changed enormously. Today you don't have one exchange with a single central limit order book, where you can see depth of liquidity. From my institutional point of view for block trading, the idea of price discovery is really more a post-trade thing than a pre-trade function.[9] You can't look at a book and say where I need to move this stock. In terms of the efficiency of a market, a lot

[9]As the speaker explained in a follow-up interview: "In a single central limit order book, like you once had and still have in some European markets, if I am a seller of say, a million shares, I can ask myself how far do I have to take the price out from the current spread? You could certainly look at it [the order] from a pre-trade perspective, because there is an incentive here in the single book on the European market to show your order. In contrast, in a multi-market [fragmented] structure like in the US, there is no benefit in exposing your hand, because other trading participants could front run you on a different exchange, or trade ahead of you. So the idea of liquidity doesn't become something you can look at in the US on a pre-trade basis. You can make assumptions based on [trading] history, but you can't make too many assumptions based on what you see in the market [pre-trade]."

of regulators and a lot of time is involved in looking at spreads in order to look at the efficiency. As spreads are tighter than they used to be, retail orders get executed at this tighter NBBO[10] or even inside it with the ability of dark ATSs, hidden liquidity in lit exchanges, and electronic liquidity providers on the OTC side all potentially offering "price improvement" to the NBBO.[11] So it appears to be a more efficient market from that point of view.

The market has developed to make it more efficient from the institutional point of view. We have more block trading tools with the growth of ECNs utilizing OMS blotter scraping technology[12] and more ATSs created with the aim of reconsolidating the block. I don't want to name any specifically, but new participants have been pretty well publicized in recent years. There are more places where we can cross blocks against counterparties. This is all part of the market developing to the state where we are in today. Now I question why some exchanges are considered an exchange, when their market share is so low? You have to be connected to them, but there is no value from an institutional trading point of view. When the revenue growth of many exchanges seems to be from connection fees, technology, and selling data, maybe the focus isn't as much on trading as it should be.

Domowitz: When you mention exchanges, one thing that comes to mind is this global movement – a diversifying away from the transaction business. In other words, the notion of price discovery at the level of the exchange has been, I want to say, subordinated. But certainly, less attention is being paid to the exchange, given the sheer economics of what is in that world. Adam's thoughts are welcome here. Adam interviews a lot of people about market structure.

Adam Sussman: One area of focus for exchanges, brokers, and everyone negatively impacted is the declining volume over the last few years. From the institutional perspective, we have heard that this other focus, which is away from the transaction business, is, in many ways, good.[13] New tools have been developed at the buy-side, bringing them on to their desktops. That is giving them more choices in how to execute.

---

[10] National Best Bid and Offer (NBBO). "National best bid and national best offer means, with respect to quotations for an NMS Security, the best bid and best offer for such security that are calculated and disseminated on a current and continuing basis by a plan processor pursuant to an effective national market system plan." Source: Code of Federal Regulations/C.F.R. § 600(b)(42).

[11] For a comprehensive account of dark pools and their opposite in lit markets, see *Dark Pools: Fear of the Dark*. Third *Way*. Lauren Oppenheimer, John Vahey. August 28, 2013. http://www.thirdway.org/report/dark-pools-fear-of-the-dark

As the authors explain: "Dark pools are private, electronic stock trading venues that allow buyers and sellers of a stock to be matched anonymously. In a dark pool, prices are not displayed to investors – stock prices are dark. Dark trading is an alternative to trading on a "lit" exchange, like the New York Stock Exchange (NYSE), where traders benefit from visible prices."

[12] This refers to allowing access to a trader's order management system, or OMS, to effectively read the trader's position he or she is aiming to execute. Liquidnet is regarded as the first system of this kind.

[13] Referring in particular to how brokers were providing more support tools on the desktops of the buy-side.

But, at the same time, there is a notion that, as the exchanges have branched out into these new areas, they have perhaps lost focus on what head traders of the institutions that we talk to believe should be their core mission: to facilitate secondary market asset allocation and price discovery. So it is a bit of a mixed bag for the industry.

Domowitz: I was reminded, and I was despairing for a while, that we didn't have enough of the customers for this panel. John, you reminded me that the sell-side are the customers of the exchanges. But the composition of this panel worked out well in the end.

John Donahue: Even though the options for execution have expanded greatly over the last 10–15 years, we are still relying on exchanges for the central point of price discovery to some extent, although not to the extent that we did maybe 15 years ago. To me, the notion of price discovery itself falls into the same category. I struggled with it in the same way; I struggled with execution quality. What does it mean? Price discovery could also mean different things to the five different people up here. I think price discovery is about technology. Technology has given us the opportunity and capability to find price discovery in different places. We access a number of different places to determine price discovery.

But, back to the exchanges. Clearly, their role has changed. Fifteen years ago, price discovery was controlled, particularly by one person, the specialist on the floor of the New York Stock Exchange. The specialist, back in the day, was standing in front of his post, with a rack of orders that only he could see, and posting the bid or offer that he wanted to post. Was that price discovery? Absolutely not, because price discovery was in the pocket of brokers who have millions of shares to buy, and you will not get that price discovery by simply hitting that bid. All I do is tip off the specialist, or the three or four brokers on the floor, that new entrants are coming to the market. Do we truly have price discovery by displaying a big bid or a big offer? I don't think so. I think today's model is more efficient. Technology has made it possible to access any number of different venues in a millisecond and determine price discovery based upon your ability to get to those destinations on your customers' behalf. So the exchanges clearly do still play a role, but the playing field has been leveled.

Domowitz: That brings up the issue of pre-trade transparency in several ways. I guess directly with respect to specialists, I sort of agree. The flip side is that there is so much data these days. It is so fast that pre-trade transparency is so complete but we can't quite get it. I'd like to ask Tim Mahoney to comment on that. The obvious ways dark pools have always been thought to be parasitic is in terms of their pricing. There is certainly truth to this by construction. But it's worth at least asking what role that type of execution has, in the context of price discovery itself.

Mahoney: On a panel like this, it is always important we appreciate the context of what we are talking about. We still have in the US, as we just discussed, the most efficient cash equity market in the world. So we need to be careful about any changes we make. And we talked about price discovery. It is a complex topic because it's really about either short-term price discovery or long-term price discovery. And how does that affect the investment process? I spent 20 years as a buy-side trader. I can tell you that trading is a piece of that puzzle. But the bigger piece, the more important piece, quite frankly, is the decisions of the portfolio manager. What stock to buy and when. And you are actualizing those ideas.

To move from the bottom quantile to the top quantile in performance in Lipper is 200 basis points. So, with price discovery, we may be very focused on mechanics. But we want to make sure we *do* not lose sight of the real goal – long-term investment performance. When I think about the dark pool debate, and on the exchange side, the question I ask is why is liquidity moving off exchanges? Does it have to do with rational or irrational participants? In that context, you start to think you have some of the smartest people in the world with regulatory obligations and, in the case of the buy-side, fiduciary obligations for best execution. And yet they are choosing to follow through and make decisions.

There are three driving factors to where we are going. The first is price discovery. I would argue that every time 50,000 or 100,000 shares trade in a venue like BIDS,[14] it is important to price discovery. We provide an important part of that. There is also price improvement, because many trades occur at the midpoint. Lastly (and this is what we often overlook), there is a real cost issue here. Internalization is, potentially, directly correlated to a reduction in commission rates.[15] You cannot take institutional commissions from 6 cents down to half of a penny or lower and take the tick size from a quarter down to a penny without consequences. If the top take fee is 28 and your client is paying you 50, 30, or 25, or whatever, you have to rationalize that cost in some way. So the dark pool is a tool for both institutions, for trade size, and for broker-dealers to provide lower cost to their end users.

When we are talking about the integrity of the marketplace, I continue to believe that we differentiate the US cash equity market from every other marketplace because of the consolidated tape in the US.[16] It's perfectly OK to have fragmentation, as long as all those trades are consolidated and reported at one place. In Europe, there is a big debate about how much dark trading they should have, and it is rather ironic because you actually don't know how dark it is given that there is no consolidated tape. The consolidated tape itself is a critically important piece of it.

[14] For more on this ATS, see the BIDS'company website http://www.bidstrading.com/about/company/

[15] A trade is internalized when it is handled and executed for an investor by the investor's "internalizing" brokerage firm, using securities held by this investor's brokerage. As a side note, brokerage firms that internalize orders can sometimes benefit from the spread, the difference between what they pay for the shares and what they sell them for.

[16] "The consolidated tape is a high-speed, electronic system that reports the latest price and volume data on sales of exchange-listed stocks. The data reflected on the consolidated tape are generated by various market centers, including all securities exchanges, electronic communications networks (ECNs), and third-market broker-dealers. Internet sites that provide updated market information and financial news programs on television often include trade reports from the consolidated tape." Source: Securities and Exchange Commission.

This statement is probably a little bolder. If you will tell me what the last sale was, and you are going to pay me in our marketplace to make quotes (because you'll get rebates). I'm not so worried about the displayed bid and offer. I will gladly be a market maker. I can see what is traded over a period of time. I can correlate those trades with everything else that occurs. I'm actually being compensated to make bids and offers. That's a decent business. So I am not sure that the displayed bid and offer is as important as a displayed last sale.

It is important to appreciate that there are other marketplaces, like fixed income. They don't have the place for displayed bids and offers, and I suspect they truly believe there is price discovery in those markets. So we fall into a trap. This is the way it works, and this is the only model. We think it is really the most efficient model, but there are a lot of other answers around that.

Sussman: Back to your question about pre-trade transparency. Pre-trade transparency and exchange trading are not always synonymous, because there are plenty of dark activities that occur on exchanges. Exchanges have dark facilities. The goal of regulators is to encourage pre-trade transparency, which we have to understand, but this does not necessarily mean shifting more order flow onto exchanges. We were looking at some slides earlier about the Canadian dark regulatory rule, which limited the amount of order flow that can be executed in the dark at a certain size, with a minimum guaranteed improvement. But there are on-exchange mechanisms within Canada that don't encourage pre-trade transparency. It seems to me like regulators in Canada only choose to ignore the lack of pre-trade transparency that happens on the exchange.

Mahoney: You can't legislate transparency on a pre-trade basis. The decision is where that order is going to be hidden. Is the order hidden in a portfolio manager's pocket? Is it hidden in the buy-side traders' pocket? Is it hidden in a broker's desk, because it is in his pocket? If you have to trade size, it's absolutely stupid to say I will buy 500 million shares or a 100,000 shares today. It can't happen. I would argue that. Because it actually provides a very effective mechanism for that to occur. Disruptive pricing is not helpful to anybody. The people who have a fiduciary obligation are making rational decisions in the most efficient marketplace in the world, and maybe we should be listening to that.

Domowitz: Many thought-provoking ideas have been exchanged in the past few minutes. Let me start first with the nature of the markets, the issue of retail. But the sense on the institutional buy-side is that they are trading in a market that is fundamentally retail, and that is a real problem. I might even say there is a problem with this for price discovery. Will and John, your thoughts from the perspective of both the buy- and sell-sides?

Donahue: The market has never been better for retail investors. The speed of execution has come down on average from over 30 s 10 years ago to sub-seconds today. The depth of the book available to the retail investor has improved. And the spreads have, of course, narrowed. We are in penny spreads now, and we used to be in quarter spreads. So, the retail experiences have been very positive. Today's market structure for the retail investor has never been better, and that's important because retail is a very important component of the overall US equity market. The flip side of that, putting on the asset managers' hat now, and going back to my role many years ago as a trader, mutual funds are made up of millions of individual investors. So all of the same things that have benefited the retail investors are also benefiting the millions of fund investors; the same efficiency that we enjoy in the market today is also benefiting the large mutual fund houses. Are there issues with market structure today? Of course, there are always issues. But, for the most part, access to liquidity and the cost of execution are both down, and the speed of execution is up. This benefits the retail investors on both sides of the business.

Lishman: From the institutional point of view, I agree. We need to have control over how we execute and where we execute. We need to be able to have control of the types of counterparties we execute against. We need things like minimum execution sizes, so we can control the footprints we leave, and so we don't transact against certain counterparties. We need the ability to take advantage of retail liquidity, by providing liquidity through algorithms. We have control. We are in a much better position than when we had to give all of our information to the floor and have someone there who could front-run you. I remember instances of trading on the floor of the New York Stock Exchange – I was at my desk, away from the change – where I joined in an offer to sell some stock. We would send an order to the broker, and the broker would send it to the floor. And it would be trading lots of volume on both the bid and offer, and we would not be getting any fills back. So I would ask "What's going on?" and be told "People ahead of you!" I'm sure it was just the specialist effectively market making ahead of institutional orders, knowing that if the market changed, the risk would be immediately transferred to the order on the book.

I used to cancel my own order to get an execution, because then the specialists would be worried his position wasn't backstopped and would fill your order. You would be told someone came in and you got filled as you cancelled, but this happened too much to be coincidence. You had to play that game. It was terrible. Now we are in a position where we have control. Talking about dark pools, there is a huge difference between dark pools which are fragmentations in the marketplace where you are getting a hundred share fills, or several hundred shares fills here and there, and those that are designed for big block executions, buy-side to buy-side, which are fantastic from the institutional point of view.

With the fragmentation of blocks and venues, execution sizes in dark pools can be smaller than the lit market, and you can be interacting with different types of liquidity than you really do not want to interact with. Again, institutional traders have control over that, but we don't always have control over these on exchanges. That still needs to be looked at. What exactly constitutes these exchanges? You have to route to somewhere that may be doing sub-one percent of the daily market volume in that stock. Is there really a benefit to what they are doing, to even entice people to come and bid and offer? They are often offering some kind of incentive too, whether it is rebates or reduced rates for increased routing, which adds to market complexity and effectively changes net prices between exchanges and isn't that friendly from an institutional point of view. When we talk about high-frequency trading (HFT) as well, the mainstream media has portrayed it all as one type of front-running firm. From an institutional point of view, most HFT is either benign or even beneficial. With market making HFT designed to trade millions of small trades every day, mainly interacting with retail investors, and the small spread crossing algorithmic transactions, being benign. And some stat arb HFT can actually be beneficial to us from a block point of view. For example, if we are trying to buy a certain stock and it moves out of line with the sector, some stat arb HFT can come in and provide liquidity in that name and hedge against the sector, potentially reducing our slippage. There is only one type of HFT that we are worried about – front-running. It's hard to know what it is as a percentage of the market. I'll say it's probably very small, as to the smallest HFT out there. Still, it is important and significant. That's why we need to keep investigating and questioning market structure and practices and keep developing extra tools and controls.

One more point. There is a difference between what I see as an efficient market and what exchanges sees as an efficient market. The exchange will see the volume, the kind of optical liquidity of what it trades. Consider an example. There are two buy-side clients, one is buying, the other is selling, a hundred thousand shares. We put them up and cross a hundred thousand shares. Now if you stop this from happening, and you make one trade with the market maker, there is another trade with the market maker now on the other side; you are doubling the volume. So the exchange is producing this optical liquidity that is two times what it is if you just allow the shares to cross. Oftentimes, they and regulators, when they look at liquidity, that's sort of what they are looking at, the total liquidity.

Well, that's not real liquidity. That's closed out, intraday, often in a very short period of time. To me an efficient market is one that puts real buyers and real sellers together. There is also a space for market making, to smooth out the timing fluctuations between buyers and sellers entering the market. I should talk about Brazil very quickly. Brazil is a one-exchange market. Everyone says that people from exchanges talk about the success of Brazil. Brazil has the other problem. They don't have any competition in terms of competition to lower fees and increase innovation. You are talking about three and a quarter basis points in exchange fees to trade. The market is actually open to having competition between exchanges, but there is only one clearing entity, and the clearer charges whatever it wants at that three and a quarter. So they make it too expensive to have another exchange.

Having one exchange actually allows them to have some good tools like iceberging. In the nature of an iceberger, you could show a 1000 shares but have a 100,000 behind it.[17] In a market where there is one exchange, you have a kind of block functionality. I can show 1000 shares and have a 100,000 or a million shares behind it. As an institution, a number of times you might have had a bid for 1500 shares and end up trading a much larger block, because you sent down an iceberged order that traded with another iceberged order on the other side.

[17] Think of the "tip of the iceberg" to further grasp this trading concept.

In my opinion, the Brazil exchange wanted to increase optical volume, and when they change their trading system, they used this to change their minimum iceberg size to 10,000 shares. This drastically reduced traders' ability to use this functionality, as you can't show many stocks in 10,00 shares, without moving the market already. This means that traders had to break up trades using algorithms increasing the ability of HFT interaction.

Domowitz: And I can tell you the costs are high in Brazil. Adam, you were looking in this direction. You want to weigh in on this?

Sussman: Among the institutional community, I don't think there is agreement that the market is better today than it was 10 years ago. When we go out and talk with asset managers, the one thing that they would all wish for, and I say which is true, is wider ticker sizes. The idea is that they don't think that going from a nickel to a penny really narrowed or improved the price discovery process, compared to what they have to go through today to get their size done. They would probably get a similar price at that size with a nickel widespread, similar to the iceberg function. It just causes them to spread the orders out, over multiple price points, over multiple sizes.

Lishman: If you look at transaction costs, they have come down. The problem is that the role of a buy-side trader has changed dramatically. We used to rely on the sell-side much more, and there was a greater sense of immediate gratification when spreads were wider, there was essentially one exchange, and so bids and offers were much larger. Now traders use a different skill set, often involving being stealthier and using multiple electronic tools – as well as some good old school sales traders – and ultimately traders are more responsible for the outcomes of their trades. Many of the heads of desks have been in the business a long time, and are nostalgic for the old days, and complain that it's a much more difficult market to trade in. But actually, even with its issues, it is much more efficient.

Sussman: Are you advocating for some kind of retirement age?

Lishman: Not at all. But it's an old school element. There is a huge diverse set of opinions on all of these things, which is part of the problem. Whenever you go to Washington as a group, the HFT community can pretty much come together and argue how efficient the market is. And the buy-side community comes with one person talking about going back to a 6 and a quarter cents spread. Someone else talks about dark pools, and someone else talks about limiting HFT. In other words, there is no one consensus. I agree with that, there isn't an answer.

Mahoney: I find the complexity argument fascinating! That today's market is more complex. Back in the day, if you traded on the New York Stock Exchange, the rules were so complex that the actual people who traded had to take a test. There were floor officials who had to take a bigger test to help interpret rules. And there were governors who were above them to help them with the rules.

Peng: What emerged from this conversation is a lot of technical details. That's very important. Different players in this game have different perspectives. From an academic point of view, what's the evidence we see from the data in terms of price discovery? In aggregate, how do investors view the cost of price discovery? Using this new measure I mentioned before, looking at the quality of prices at 10 o'clock (half an hour after the opening of the trading), we are able to classify stocks by their intraday autocorrelations. Every month we take all the stocks traded in the US, NYSE, NASDAQ, AMEX, and all the other stock exchanges. We classify them into ten groups, sorting by their intraday autocorrelation. We see that it is a pretty dispersed distribution of autocorrelations.

We look at the 10% of the stocks that have the most negative intraday autocorrelation (which is somewhere around −47%) and the 10% of the stocks that have the highest intraday autocorrelation (the correlations are positive, on the order of about 40%). We see very strong intraday price reversals, as well as a lot of intraday price continuity. We see that prices, as of 10 o'clock, either severely undershoot or overshoot the values they close at. Should investors and portfolio managers care about this, when they are thinking about their investment decisions? Should they care about these imprecisions in price discovery, this overshooting, and undershoot?

If you see this overshooting or undershootings only with crashes like a flash crash (which is a rare event), maybe they shouldn't be so concerned about it. But if there is a systematic pattern, if prices persistently under- or overshoots, then perhaps it is a serious concern for the customers. In our study, we sort the stocks by their intraday autocorrelation patterns into ten groups, and we look at their expected returns (i.e., the required rate of return, the expected return investors would require on these stocks over time). We looked at a fairly long period of time. We look at all the data from 1993 to 2010.[18] So we have 17 years of data. We see from the data that investors require a risk premium of about 54 basis points per month for stocks that have the greatest overshooting, compared to stocks that have the highest undershooting. So that is the average cost of price discovery over these 17 years period. Going back to John's point concerning technology advances and innovations, from your perspective, we seem to have improved price discovery. If we compare the sample prior to decimalization in 2001 with the sample post-decimalization, we indeed see a cost reduction on price discovery. Pre-decimalization, the cost of price discovery, is about 74 basis points per month. Post-decimalization, it is about 36 basis points a month. The reduction is dramatic, but the premium has nevertheless remained highly significant, at about 36 basis points per month. Translating that into an annualized return, it's about 4.4% per year.

Domowitz: I find that very interesting. That's partly because the over-/undershooting is relative to the close, so there is certainly a presumption that the close represents true value. It also tells me that Vanguard actually should be producing a lot of alpha, given market on close trading activities. I don't want to debase this at all; it's just to put it in context with what we say in terms of the cost.

[18] The analysis was subsequently expanded to include the years through 2014.

And here is a follow-up question: There were talks about dark pools being block trading facilities (originally by design), and that is absolutely correct. And certainly the average trade size in dark pools now, if you look across all of them, it's quite small, more or less what is likely also seen on an exchange. So Lin Peng, when you think about price discovery, and you think about quantity discovery (which is usually what's talked about as being a benefit), in your mind, is there a difference? And if so, what does it look like, and is it meaningful?

Peng: I think quantity discovery is an important part of price discovery. I would like to look to see if the data are available. We would love to see what the data looks like, in terms of price discovery in the dark pools, and compare that with the current study that just looks at the prices.

Domowitz: As an academic, I would point out that overshooting and undershooting may have something to do with order size. That's the essential part of the dark pool debate, and it certainly should be a central thing here.

Bob Schwartz [From the Floor]: I'd like to bring quantity discovery into the picture discovery. In economics courses, we talk about demand and supply. It is a simultaneous solution, quantity discovery, and price discovery. One aspect of efficiency to consider is the extent to which those two have decoupled in our current environment.

Domowitz: I agree completely. The debate itself has also decoupled them. That's one of the reasons I ask this question. In my mind, they don't deserve to be decoupled. We have somehow managed to separate them.

Switching gears, we've talked a lot about intra-market competition – competition in a market for markets in terms of the exchange that was brought out very well in a speech on behalf of the World Federation of Exchanges.[19] Certainly competition for order flow among exchanges and alternative trading venues one way or another, I would call that intra-market. Inter-market, in my mind, is relevant to price discovery. Frankly, we have been complaining a lot about the fragmentation of the markets and about the technology involved in it. But it actually has coupled. Take the derivatives markets; they are much more closely in design to the equity markets today. Would you view that as favorable in the context of price discovery? I'll take a volunteer, audience, or panelist.

Sussman: Look, for example, at markets where you have an exchange-traded instrument, but where the underlying is not traded on an exchange. A good example would be the proliferation of corporate bond exchange-traded funds, or ETFs. For investors' preferences, they have been growing in assets under management, and they trade on an exchange or across the entire US equity market structure. But the underlying, the bonds themselves, still trade off exchange in probably the

[19] See Chap. 2: A Global Perspective. Huseyin Erkan, CEO, World Federation of Exchanges.

darkest pools you could imagine. Statistical hedge funds and high-frequency trading bring efficiency to the pricing of the ETFs, by trading across both the bond and ETF markets. We are seeing some of the institutional accounts look at the corporate bond market who say, "when interest rates rise and we need to offload these securities, we will need a better path. The banks can no longer take on the inventory they did in the past because of capital regulations." The point is that they – the institutional accounts – see the corporate bond ETF as a competitor to their active managed bond portfolios. But they also see it as an instigator and as a way to move the corporate bond market to be more liquid and more transparent. So, if you take that extreme example, I think there are similarities in even some of the more liquid instruments, where both the derivative and the underlying trade on exchanges.

Domowitz: How does that work out for you Tim?

Mahoney: I agree. The proliferation of ETFs has brought that correlation higher. So it is most obvious when we have a problem with the SIP,[20] and basically the entire world has almost shut down. That helps particularly in hedging. ETFs have a lot of valuable input and market. I think it causes some problems, too.

Domowitz: I would add to your market-consolidated tape remarks that it seems to work reasonably well here, but you have to report your ETFs. It's a bit of a problem in the European Union but, more broadly, even in terms of the relationship between equities and FX, bonds, futures, and options. Are we seeing any benefits in terms of price discovery there?

Mahoney: Technology has been a big aid to that. I remember trading international stocks and trying to do FX. You needed the precise settlement details before you could do the FX part of the trade. Because of the delay between trading the stock and getting the confirm, you had to wait 35–40 min. Now everything is becoming more efficient today, and the market is clearly more correlated. I don't know how much of that is because of market structure and how much is technology. My feeling is that it is more technology based because it moves faster and faster and things are understood quicker. There is higher correlation in the marketplaces.

Domowitz: Yes. Back to the network I introduced earlier today. Will?

---

[20] "The Security Information Processor (SIP) links the US markets by processing and consolidating all protected bid/ask quotes and trades from every trading venue into a single, easily consumed data feed." Source: Consolidated Tape Association.

More broadly, NASDAQ and NYSE, at time of writing, each operated a SIP for US stock exchanges. These data processors consolidate quote and trade data for stocks listed on their exchanges. The data is then disseminated for a fee to investors, market data providers, and others. NYSE also operated a SIP for options exchanges.

Lishman: When you look at integrated price discovery from an academic point of view, I don't know how you take into account other changes to market dynamics that have occurred recently, like the velocity of capital which is much, much faster than it used to be. And then there's the velocity of news dissemination today.

Peng: In our statistical work, we do control for volatility in various ways.

Lishman: In terms of ETFs, we trade the bond ETFs for some of our multi-asset strategies, which is interesting because you have a very transparent ETF made on a product with very opaque underlying liquidity. It is surprisingly liquid and trades very much like an equity for small and medium size, but because there isn't efficiency in the creation/redemption basket, it trades much more like a bond for large size. In general, the market is healthy; it is much more efficient than it used to be, with the interconnectivity between markets, like futures and cash equities, allowing almost instant arbitrage, which has the result of tightening spreads. But there are issues with that; the interconnectedness can cause problems when there is an issue with quoting or an issue with liquidity. And you can have these kinds of crazy moves in terms of market integrity.

We need to do something about it. It doesn't give people a warm, fuzzy feeling if they suddenly see a stock drop from 100 dollars to 10 cents or something else. From an institutional point of view, we protect our clients by sending orders down with constraints, so that we are trading within the tolerance band that we think is acceptable, based on intraday volatility, or the standard deviation of moves we would expect. So that, in a flash crash scenario, our algorithms will not participate in extreme adverse moves.

Domowitz: I'm seeing some evolution on the sell-side, the consolidation of multi-asset classes, even with the technology.

Donahue: Aside from the addition of retail investors into derivatives, I keep saying that 15 years ago, prior to the advance of technology and the Internet, giving investors market data at their fingertips, most retail investors tended to stay away from complex instruments. Look at the earning statements of any of the public-traded online brokers, and you will see that options trading probably is the leading growth product. And that opens up the whole new area of interest for market participants, if you have dislocations that can cause it.

Domowitz: There's a question from the floor.

David Craw: [Chairman of ISA]. The trend that we've noticed here is of lower tick sizes and lower available liquidity. At the same time, we've seen issuers like Google maintaining a high price, over $850 a share, and Apple at $480. To what extent do you think that's the effect of today's market liquidity or stock splits?

Domowitz: From an academic point of view, there is a huge volume of literature on stock splits. The reason that they are interesting is because nothing is supposed to happen if you split a stock. That's also true in principle if you have reverse splits. We took a long hard look at the Citi Group experience.[21] And there are some answers to that. In the reverse split case, I think I can say with reasonable confidence that the market actually became better for what is considered retail-size orders. On the other hand, large institutional orders on a reverse split actually suffered, but that's a complex story in itself. The only thing I like to echo in terms of the question is that there are effects, and we should think about that.

That wraps up a superb panel discussion. Thank you.

[21] See Trading Patterns, Liquidity, and the Citigroup Split. Milan Borkovec, Ian Domowitz, and Konstantin Tyurin. The *Journal of Trading*. 19. *Fall 2011* http://www.iijournals.com/doi/pdfplus/10.3905/jot.2011.6.4.018

Chapter 4
Integrity of a Marketplace

Bob Pisani, Joe Bonocore, Gary Katz, John Kelly, Keith Ross, and Oakley E. (Lee) Van Slyke

Robert Schwartz: It is with much enthusiasm that I once again warmly welcome Bob Pisani to Baruch College for our conference today. Bob, it is a pleasure to see you here.

Bob Pisani: I have participated in this great annual conference so many times over the years. I must admit, it's one of my favorite industry gatherings. We will discuss marketplace integrity on this panel. And I will open with a question for a 10,000-feet view.

As background, Dan Gallagher, a Commissioner at the Securities and Exchange Commission, recently told me his major goal for the year when I interviewed him on the air.[1] He said he would like a big sky review of market structure, an overall review. Of course, that's a clear invitation to bury market structure at the SEC. Because you know it will result in a major report – in 3 years, and by then it will be out of date!

[1] Daniel (Dan) Gallagher, SEC Commissioner, November 2011 to October 2015.

B. Pisani (✉)
CNBC, Englewood Cliffs, NJ, USA

J. Bonocore
Citigroup, New York, NY, USA

G. Katz
International Securities Exchange, New York, NY, USA

J. Kelly
Liquidnet, New York, NY, USA

K. Ross
PDQ Enterprises LLC, New York, NY, USA

O. E. (Lee) Van Slyke
Extraordinary Re, San Clemente, CA, USA

© Springer Nature Switzerland AG 2019
R. A. Schwartz et al. (eds.), *Market Integrity*, Zicklin School of Business Financial Markets Series, https://doi.org/10.1007/978-3-030-02871-8_4

So Gary, start us off. What is right and what is not right about market structure, specifically, for example, with Reg NMS?[2] If you were emperor of the market structure world, what would you change?

Gary Katz: Wow, I'd love to be the emperor! I would first tell the SEC they should just hire Steve Wunsch.[3] He'll explain it all to them! Then they'll know everything on the topic of Reg NMS. I would also note that there is no one or two simple ideas that will fix everything. Part of the problem is that everybody is looking for the one item they could remove from a very complicated market structure. In doing that, the thinking is that it would somehow solve all the problems we've been discussing at this and at many other conferences.

Since the topic of this panel is the integrity of a marketplace, I would say, do not fix anything. Instead, present what we already have as being much better than how it is portrayed today by the media and the public. We have fantastic capital markets; they are the envy of the world. We should talk about what works in our markets, not about what doesn't work.

I'm reminded of a study of two bowling teams by a group of professionals. They studied how they bowled for one full game. For one team, they pointed out all the mistakes they had made while bowling; for the other, they pointed out all the things that they were doing really well. Then they all bowled again. The team handed the negative instructions and lecture on what they were doing wrong did worse the second time around. The team that was told what they were doing well did better.

Many of us who are managers would say that's the right way to manage people who work for us. Don't always point out the things they're doing wrong; try to point out what they're doing right. The capital markets of the United States are doing far more things right than they are doing wrong. We've spent too much time pointing out the things that are wrong.

Pisani: Keith Ross, your thoughts? Is market efficiency better than it was 20 years ago? I've been with CNBC for 24 years and at the New York Stock Exchange since 1996.[4] The minute I got here, the first thing I found out is that everybody hated the specialists. The buy-side despised the specialists and thought they were ripping them off. But I found out that the buy-side has always hated the sell-side since I got into market history. My whole life down there on the NYSE floor still, to a certain extent, consists of the buy-side screaming, "Pisani, do you know what the Coke specialist did to me today. Let me just tell you!" Now that's not as big a thing as it used to be. But the sell-side was always complaining about what was going on. Are things any better today than they were 20 years ago?

---

[2] Reg NMS (Regulation National Market System) was adopted by the Securities and Exchange Commission in 2005 and introduced 2 years later to further advance the ideals of a national market system. The regulation includes the order protection, or trade-through rule, access rule (fair access) to market data including quotations, and rules on sub-penny trading and on market data.

[3] Founder of the now defunct Arizona Stock Exchange, an electronic stock exchange, the headquarters of the company was based in New York. A former Kidder Peabody vice president, Wunsch is also known for his expertise and knowledge of market structure and for his free enterprise outlook.

[4] Bob Pisani is a news correspondent for financial news network CNBC and covers the New York Stock Exchange from the floor.

Keith Ross: The short answer is yes. We heard that from panelists earlier in the day. Knight Capital Group published a 2013 update of a 2010 market study that catalogued the display and impact of orders in the marketplace. The takeaway is that markets are deeper and the costs of transactions, for retail and institutional investors, are lower than before.[5] The study had about 17 metrics in terms of display size, liquidity size, and market impact. The study is very comfortable in showing that the markets are better today and that they continue to improve. I once believed the high-frequency trading, or HFT, professionals, who replaced the specialists, took the venom that was previously fired at the specialists. But we may have to reevaluate that.

I think the markets are highly efficient, that the cost to execute is low, and that market impact is low. I like to go back to what the regulators were hoping for in 2005 when they introduced Reg NMS.[6] They wanted a more competitive, more efficient, and a faster market. They got much more than they ever thought possible.

An interesting project might be this: A study to help us decide if we want to remain where we are at today. The one thing I might tweak is the tick size for various types of priced equities. Because I think it is too small today for the big ones and maybe too big for the small ones. That is being discussed and considered.[7]

Pisani: Anybody else want to tweak anything in the current market structure? Is everybody really happy about things?

Joe Bonocore: I agree that the markets are much more efficient now than they were, say 20 years ago. I think the markets right now are at an inflection point. For the first time in a generation, markets have been straddling the fixed income and equity markets. But do I really want to be involved in fixed income now, since the only direction for rates is up? And how do I feel about the absolute level of where the equity markets are? How do I make that decision about where I should be investing my money, and should I be trading? The markets overall though are definitely more efficient.[8]

---

[5] Equity Trading in the twenty-first Century: An Update James J. Angel, Georgetown University. Lawrence E. Harris, University of Southern California. Chester S. Spat, Carnegie Mellon University (June 06, 2013, Knight Capital Group).

[6] See 2.

[7] Referring to a proposed pilot program for trading small-cap stocks in wider minimum increments. The pilot eventually was approved by the Securities and Exchange Commission. See *SEC Approves Pilot Program to Assess Tick Size Impact for Smaller Companies.* Center for Financial Stability, May 7, 2015. http://centerforfinancialstability.org/wp/?p=5987

[8] 2013 continued to see falling interest rates following the 2008 financial crisis. Consequently, falling rates had allowed the value of bonds to increase as yields declined. Bond prices move inversely to interest rates as is well known. With short-term rates in 2013 at almost zero, and long-term rates at record lows, it was practically impossible for rates to dip any further. As 2013 progressed, rates started to climb. Rising rates would ultimately translate into meager yields but also losses of principal, according to financial experts. The Dow Jones industrial average had a banner year in 2013, its best since 1998, gaining 26.5%; the NASDAQ soared 38%. Meanwhile, investors were taking flight from bonds, pulling over $70 billion from bond mutual funds, according to TrimTabs, by one measure in December 2013. See Stock: 2013 is one for the record books. Ben Rooney. CNNMoney.com. December 31, 2013. http://buzz.money.cnn.com/2013/12/31/stocks-record-bull-market/Stock

Pisani: John Kelly, all dark pools are not created equal. This is sort of the motto of Liquidnet?

John Kelly: Actually, that's quoting Mary Schapiro, former chairman of the SEC.

Pisani: All right. Years ago, we had block trading desks; now we have dark pools. Are dark pools contributing to price discovery?[9] Please talk a little bit about your aspect of the business.

Kelly: I will say a couple of things that might sound contrary to an operator of a dark pool. Our interests often align with many of the exchanges and their regulators. Liquidnet is a global institutional trading network that enables over 800 asset managers to trade across 42 markets, using technology to protect their orders and minimize market impact. High-frequency trading, or HFT, is definitely a hot button issue for our global network members, who at best are evenly divided on the topic. Regulators are mainly concerned about trading that takes place in the non-displayed markets (also known as dark pools) that don't contribute to price discovery. Another concern is how high-frequency trading players take advantage of market structure.

Liquidnet believes that, from the beginning, industry participants and regulators understood the value of the wholesale market. Professional traders needed a way to trade large-size orders (also known as "blocks"), without significantly moving the price. At the time, block orders placed in the "pit" or open outcry system would immediately move the price at the time of trade and, thereby, disadvantage all investors including the retail market.[10]

The original idea of block trading was to trade without disrupting pricing in the open market. We believe that dark pool technology serves its intended purpose by protecting orders and minimizing market impact. Liquidnet is supportive of regulatory efforts that encourage dark pool trading, as long as the trade is large in scale and demonstrates meaningful price improvement. If not, we believe that the trade is best fit for the displayed market.

[9] For a comprehensive account of dark pools and their opposite in lit markets, see Dark Pools: Fear of the Dark. Third Way. Lauren Oppenheimer, John Vahey. August 28, 2013.

http://www.thirdway.org/report/dark-pools-fear-of-the-dark. The authors explain: "Dark pools are private, electronic stock trading venues that allow buyers and sellers of a stock to be matched anonymously. In a dark pool, prices are not displayed to investors—stock prices are dark. Dark trading is an alternative to trading on a 'lit' exchange, like the New York Stock Exchange (NYSE), where traders benefit from visible prices."

[10] "Pit" and "open outcry" are synonymous. Open outcry is a broader name for any exchange-based trading on a traditional exchange floor, though the term pit has an implied association with the futures and options markets in Chicago. Traditional specialists operated on the floor, and in what's known as the upstairs market, where brokers work larger-size orders between each other. Liquidnet says its model most closely resembles block trading in the upstairs market but also differs, by expanding access from just brokers to also asset managers and related professional wholesale market participants.

Today, there are more than 40 dark pools in the equity markets. The average execution size in all of those pools is around 200 shares. The New York Stock Exchange's average trade size is 250 shares; NASDAQ is a little less than that. Trades of that size perform best in the displayed market and can contribute to both liquidity and price discovery.

Pisani: Your point is that you're different at Liquidnet. And while dark pools were originally created for one purpose, to protect block trades, high-frequency traders have subsequently crept into the marketplace. And as we all know, trade size has decreased dramatically over the years since dark pool trading was made available.

Kelly: It's not just high-frequency traders. The sell-side and, indeed, the buy-side take advantage of the liquidity that's facilitated through dark pools. Liquidnet alone trades over 1.3 billion shares per day on its platform.[11]

Pisani: Dark pool and internalized volume seem very high by comparison to exchange volume. What happens if dark pool trading goes to 50 or 60% of total equity market share? When I talk to institutional traders, they say they are very concerned about being picked off by high-frequency traders. Are these traders inherently abusing the market?

Kelly: There are always bad actors in the markets or in any economic activity for that matter. It's true that as soon as a trading desk starts firing on all cylinders, taking advantage of high-power computing, algorithmic trading strategies, and reduced latencies through co-location, it's possible to not only maximize trading efficiencies but to trigger new trading opportunities. The increase in trading activity starts to cross over to all market participants. This is what the regulators want to be mindful of as the market continues to evolve.

Pisani: Has the proliferation of dark pools and alternative trading systems had an impact on market integrity overall? It's interesting to note how trading costs have dramatically reduced since the advent of technology. Currently, as an example, it's only $7.95 to do 1000 shares of IBM today. Twenty years ago, it would have cost over $300 for the same 1000 shares of IBM. But are there any hidden costs as a result of electronic trading?

Kelly: Most dark pool operators charge commissions and include rebates as incentives to participate. We believe its best that pricing is driven from the market, rather than regulators using pricing as a way to influence or to modify market behavior. I'm a fan of principles-based regulation that allows institutional market participants to decide who they will trade with and why.[12] This flexibility allows them to honor

[11] 2016 data supplied by Liquidnet.

[12] Principles-based regulation is the concept of regulation that lays our broad but clearly defined principles that business is expected to follow, in contrast to rules-based regulation that defines what is right and wrong and the boundaries of the law.

their fiduciary obligation to their stakeholders, such as mutual or pension fund managers, or even retail or private capital market participation. We're comfortable about the investment manager making the choices presented by the market, consistent with well-developed principles-based regulation.

Pisani: Something seems out of whack to me. The reason it's more expensive on an exchange is that you've got to pay for a lot more. I mean you have to pay for surveillance technology, for customer support, for somebody to answer the phone. If dark pools get all the good order flow, then does the floor get all the toxic order flow? If so, does that distort the exchange structure overall?

Katz: Go back a little in time, you can see that that's exactly what happened. The buy-side used to complain about the specialists all the time. And we've heard this a number of times: Wouldn't it be great if we just went back to trading stocks in nickels rather than in decimals, and then we could have the specialists back again. Of course, it all depends on your perspective and on where you sit.

There were once many specialists on the floor of the NYSE. And these specialists are now no longer in business. One reason why is that they once could trade with a mix of flow – some of it was this toxic flow we talk about. But some of it was the retail flow that they were able to make money on. Making money is not a bad thing. It allows you to interact with the entire mix of business. When that retail business is removed from the mix, you're left with a very difficult situation. How do you continuously fill the screens with two-sided quotes if nobody wants to make that market? They know that they're about to get run over. The answer that was developed was maker-taker.[13] In the past, NYSE specialists, when they put a quote up for display on the screen, would pay the exchange a fee in the process of actually providing liquidity that is postings bids and offers.[14] Today, in order to have liquidity provided, you have to pay somebody to provide that same liquidity. But when you do, somebody else has to pay – and it's a taker fee to cover the cost of the maker.[15] And that's what I meant by there being no one simple market structure change that will improve or let's say "fix" the marketplace. It's a complex weave that we've created here. There is no one thread sticking out that's wrong. They're all connected to each other. You'd have to unwind the whole thing and build it back up from scratch.

Pisani: What's the difference between the equities market structure and the options market structure?

---

[13] A program promoted by exchanges to encourage trading on their individual exchanges. Maker-taker fees offer a transaction rebate to trading participants who provide liquidity, charging customers who take liquidity.

[14] In a follow-up interview, Katz, for clarity, noted that he was talking about options trading and that the "fee" was charged on a per share or per contract basis.

[15] Ibid.

Katz: From a market structure perspective, there's an enormous difference between options and equities. The biggest difference is that there are no dark pools in options by rule.[16] There is no place where you can match an order and then just print it on a TRF in the options market.[17] It's something that was a red line in the sand for the SEC.[18] The SEC will allow certain guarantees of interaction with order flow up to a percentage, say 40%. But the balance of the order needs to be exposed to the crowd. Even the 40% guarantee needs to be exposed to the crowd, whether it's a floor or an electronic crowd, to allow the potential for price improvement. As a result, all flow goes to exchanges in the options market. There is no fragmentation. Maybe a better word for fragmentation would be internalization. There is no opportunity to internalize the good flow that you want to trade with and then leave the balance of the flow for somebody else to deal with. In options, it all has to go to the exchange.

Pisani: Joe, you're in a somewhat different space here. You do debt issuance and securitization over at Citigroup. What are your thoughts on securitization these days? During the financial crisis, a lot of the securitization market seemed to have shut down.[19] It's back with a vengeance now; fixed-income investors are out there, and they're hungry for yield. Should I stay in my high-yield funds? That is one of the most common e-mails I get. Debt issuances are oversubscribed. We're watching a huge year in debt and a huge year in secondaries. The secondary market is just doing fabulously, arguably better than the IPO market which gets all the glory. Nobody ever pays attention to secondaries. But that's where the real business is if you look at the capital markets.

---

[16] See 9.

[17] "Trade Reporting Facilities, commonly called TRFs, are venues for alternative execution facilities to report trades to the consolidated tape. ECNs and brokers, executing stock trades away from the exchanges in the US must report their trades to a TRF. Originally, all broker dealers internalized stock trades, and as well as crossing networks and ECNs that matched trades from their customers, had to report their trades to the National Association of Securities Dealers (NASD), via the NASDAQ Stock Market's Automated Confirmation Transaction System, known as ACT.

"However, as a condition for the US Securities and Exchange Commission's approval of NASDAQ's application to register as a national stock exchange, and separate from its regulator, the NASD, the SEC insisted there be a separate TRF within the NASD. This opened the doors for other exchanges to create TRFs with the NASD, and to atttact trade printing income." Source: Markets Wiki.

[18] In a follow-up, Katz noted: "The reason that the SEC does not touch this is that stocks are issued by a company, while options are issues by the Options Clearing Corp (OCC). The OCC is owned by the exchanges, and so they would not support options being traded off exchange. If they traded off exchange, they would not be fungible with the options cleared by OCC. I believe that the SEC would want everything traded on exchange but the genie is out of the bottle in equities. They would not make that same mistake in options."

[19] The well-documented global financial crisis of 2007 and 2008, tied in the United States to subprime mortgage lending. As a reminder, the fall of Lehman Brothers, a global banking behemoth, in September 2008, almost brought the world's financial system to its knees. The worse recession in 80 years followed, but it took massive amounts of fiscal stimulus in the United States to avoid a downward economic spiral, according to financial historians.

What do the average investors do with their money when rates are rising? I know this is not a market structure issue, but you're the guy who knows a lot about this?

Bonocore: It kind of comes back to what I was saying earlier about the market being at an inflection point.[20] Typically, if you're thinking about economic value, the last thing you really want to do as an investor is to build up a large fixed-income book if you believe that rates are going to rise. If the price comes down, you're going to have an economic loss. At the same time, investors like the concept of being able to clip a coupon and have some certainty about how much interest they're earning from their investments. It's sort of their safety net, their cushion.

But those markets have been on a rollercoaster. Bob [Pisani], as you said, during the crisis, the securitization market all but shut down. Nobody wanted to touch the paper. There wasn't a whole lot of appetite to hold that type of paper, issued primarily by financial institutions which were in the doghouse. Debt issuance still carried on, but it was conducted with wide spreads that the market had never seen before.

I remember when I started doing this. You could issue a piece of senior unsecured debt out of a holding company, if you had a decent rating at single-digit basis points above LIBOR.[21] I believe that Citigroup issued something around 500 basis points above LIBOR during the depths of the crisis. I was at JPMorgan at the time. Still, you were talking about 250, 300 basis points above LIBOR, and for securitizations you just couldn't even do it.

So things have changed for the better. And at Citigroup we've a balance sheet that we need to fund. Secondaries are really where all the business is. All we're doing is issuing the initial bonds, and then the market is trading them. When we talk about market efficiency, those secondaries have bounced all over the place, particularly when you get into things like preferred stock. I don't know what the spread should be. I know what the 10-year treasury is. Does the market look at a perpetual preferred as a 10-year, because it has an option?

Does it look at it as a 30-year because they don't think we're going to call the preferred stock on the option date? The only thing we could do is start issuing and seeing how the secondaries behave.

And, when I talk about efficiencies in the market from my perspective, there are a lot of questions that I think are unanswered. Regulators have a lot to do with it.

Pisani: What would that do to the valuation of debt? Would it drive interest rates up? Would it drive up the price of existing debt now? Does that make investors worried about buying debt now?

Bonocore: I think so. A lot of the questions we hear at our fixed-income investor reviews concern where the government is going to go. There is obviously a lot of talk out there, under the so-called orderly liquidation authority that will require a

[20] See 8.

[21] London Interbank Offered Rate used by some large banks to calculate interest rates on various loans and also used as the benchmark rate some large global banks charge each other on loans.

minimum amount of long-term debt to be held by banks, based on some formula.[22] The view is that there will be a minimum amount. Depending on what that minimum amount is, could banks fall short? Could we see a situation where this is what investors are thinking? Where the banks need to literally flood the market with some exorbitant amount of long-term debt?

Whenever that happens, what would banks do to raise that kind of debt? Do we think that those levels, combined with interest rates rising, will result in long-term debt being issued at significant rates? That is to say, significantly higher rates than they are today? Obviously if that happens, the secondary market changes, and then the value of what investors hold depreciates. Nobody wants that. There is a lot of uncertainty out there. And I think the reason why you can't necessarily look at secondaries as a benchmark anymore is for that reason – too much uncertainty.

Pisani: Lee runs Extraordinary Re, a firm that is looking to create a marketplace for liquid insurance liability contracts.[23] Lee, you're doing something very interesting. I didn't even know you had a marketplace for that. Tell us a bit about that business. Is the actuarial profession actually studying liquidity? What have you figured out?

Lee Van Slyke: Let me take the second question first about the actuarial community. Insurance risks by their very nature are not liquid. They're not transferrable because insurance regulators want the insurance company that wrote a commitment to honor it later. So, they are highly illiquid in the natural market where they arise. On the other hand, accounting regulations, particularly in the US, have changed to emphasize a need to have, at least as a backstop, an estimate of the market value or to be able to mark to market.[24] In other words, to adjust to book value up or down, according to the change in the market value. But we don't have market values for insurance liabilities. We are the big outlier in the financial contracts world. Almost every other kind of significant class of financial contracts now has liquidity and the ability to reach the capital markets. Insurance liabilities don't have this liquidity. It's a hard problem. There are very good reasons why they don't as of now.

---

[22] The orderly liquidation provision in the Dodd-Frank law empowers regulators to seize a major financial firm that is headed for collapse and dismantle it in a way that is less disruptive than either taxpayer-funded bailouts or bankruptcy.

See *FDIC Initiatives under the Dodd-Frank Wall Street Reform and Consumer Protection Act.* https://www.fdic.gov/regulations/reform/initiatives.html

[23] See *Insurance Liabilities Could Be Next Big Thing for Investors. Start up Extraordinary Re is bringing much-needed change to the insurance industry by securitizing underserved risks.* Julie Segal, *Institutional Investor*. September 21, 2016. http://www.institutionalinvestor.com/article/3587123/investors-endowments-and-foundations/insurance-liabilities-could-be-next-big-thing-for-investors.html?ArticleId=3587123&p=1#/.WNvnatQrLvZ

[24] In GAPP, or Generally Accepted Accounting Principles, some income streams have to be adjusted when there are changes in their market value. There are exemptions such as certain inventories and bonds bought to be held to maturity. In an insurance company, any changes in the market value of a stock portfolio held for investment have to be factored into the income calculations of the insurance company, a process which is referred to marking the income "to market" (or "marked to market").

What the actuarial profession discovered is a great big difference between the bid and the ask.[25] Basically, we're running a business where the value of the liabilities to the party holding it are substantially different than to the people investing in the stock of the insurance operations.[26]

Two years ago, Todd Bault, an analyst at Citigroup, did a tabulation of the market capitalization of the reinsurance industry globally compared to the book value. Bault found that the market caps of these companies were 68% of the book value of the reinsurance companies. So, if you started a reinsurance company 10 years ago, then as of 2 years ago, you would have destroyed 32% of your investment on average; maybe you did worse than average. Now, the difference doesn't come from the valuation of stocks and bonds; it comes from the valuation of the insurance liabilities.

There is a huge mismatch between the valuation of the liabilities in these illiquid balance sheets and the market value that the capital markets perceive for these balance sheets. Our goal is to create liquidity for the liabilities and insurance balance sheets so that we can close that gap.[27] Either find out that the companies ought to be valued higher or find out that the liabilities, in fact, are understated and should be valued higher.

Pisani: Why is it the last major class of financial contracts that has never been securitized?

Van Slyke: Three distinct qualities of insurance liabilities make them very hard to securitize. One is that insurance liabilities must have an impeccable counterparty. If Jim Ross were to sell me an insurance policy, I know it would be really good. If Joe Rosen were to sell me an insurance policy, I might wonder (laughter)![28] The quality of the counterparty is really, really important, and so there are tons of regulations about that.

The second is that these liabilities are enormously volatile. If you had an asset that you were valuing on your books at $4 million, and it suddenly went to $400, you'd think you had a really big valuation problem. But it's not unusual for an unearned premium reserve for a homeowner's policy to be valued at $400. And then suddenly there's a flood, and now you've say a $4 million loss. These are really

[25] Referring to the idea that the insured party, say a municipality which oversees a major public water dam, inherently knows much more about the specific risk scenarios of the insured risk, than outside parties, most notably the insurance company underwriting the risk.

[26] Ibid.

[27] In practical terms, as one analyst noted, the Extraordinary Re electronic platform would offer more transparency, more liquidity, and a more accurate reflection of risk and supply in this otherwise "opaque" marketplace today. Big insurers would have a benchmark for their next deal derived from information gathered over time on insurance risk factors and as shares of insurance contracts are traded on the platform.

[28] Van Slyke is jokingly taking these two well-known Wall Street practitioners to make his point, the first practitioner held out here being a low risk, the second a high risk! (Rosen, the latter practitioner, is affiliated with Extraordinary Re.)

volatile, even in the aggregate. They're volatile because thousands of homes can all be destroyed in a single storm. Take another example: Product liability might affect thousands of patients that have taken a particular drug or implant. The nature of the risk is that these things are truly volatile liabilities.

Finally, the natural contracts that arise in insurance are heterogeneous. They're not like coffee futures where you try to get a particular country's coffee, with a particular grade and all of that (a very homogeneous thing). The natural contracts in insurance combine all kinds of timing differences, property versus liability, different state governments, different laws in which they will be adjudicated. That's a real problem. It has been an unsolvable problem up until now.

Pisani: Can you tell me how many contracts are actually being securitized? Is there a number value for the kind of progress you're making on this?

Van Slyke: The industry as a whole has certainly made some progress. Take certain kinds of contracts – for example, aggregate stop loss contracts, when the total liability gets bigger than a certain number, which cede a part of a liability. They have been turned into catastrophe bonds. Bonds, of course, are a kind of security. And transforming a liability into a security is called securitization. These aggregate stop loss contracts aggregate the losses for a number of different things. And if the total losses exceed the threshold set out in the contract, called the attachment point, then the insurance or reinsurance company is responsible for a stated part of the amount by which the losses exceed the attachment point.

So it is the part of the total losses of some threshold. Certain specialty risks have been put into what have been called sidecars that are special purpose reinsurance companies.[29] But today that's still small. If there is $40 billion worth of securitizations today, that's out of multiple tens of trillions of dollars of liability. So, it's zero if you round it off to three significant figures – that is, $40 billion divided by $22 trillion dollars equals zero if you round it off to three significant figures.

We are still a startup company. We haven't securitized anything yet. But the soft market for it is in the extraordinary risks, where the actuarial methods of doing valuation just don't work.

Pisani: Let me switch subjects. I want to talk about some of the technology glitches we have seen recently. This is what gets our viewers crazed. We've seen them at the NYSE, NASDAQ, Facebook, and Knight Trading.[30] How do you view

[29] A reinsurance sidecar, sometimes referred to as a reinsurance sidecar vehicle or simply a sidecar, is a financial structure established to allow investors (often external or third-party) to take on the risk and benefit from the return of specific books of insurance or reinsurance business. Source: www.Artemis.bm

[30] Aug. 1 stock trading fiasco costs Knight $604M, USA Today, October 17, 2012. According to the opening paragraph in this AP story: "The Knight Capital Group trading firm said it lost $764.3 million in the third quarter because of a software glitch that flooded the stock market with trades one day in August, causing dozens of stocks to fluctuate wildly." http://www.usatoday.com/story/money/markets/2012/10/17/knight-capital-earnings/1638817/

these technology glitches? Are they a natural consequence of the fact that increasing complexity increases risks? Is that the way we should look at it? Is it evidence that the system is broken? What should we tell our viewers when things of this kind happen?

Katz: The word I would use is inevitable. They were going to happen and will continue to happen. I agree with SEC Chairman, Mary Jo White, that we should have a zero tolerance goal. But in the meeting held with the CEOs of the exchanges and the clearing houses, White was very open with us. She said that system breakdowns will happen.

The question is: How do we handle ourselves as an industry when it does? How can we work together to ensure that the customer has the best experience possible? How do we try to limit the number of these events, coming out of single point of failure systems? We can try to have as much redundancy as possible across the industry, but with a clear understanding that computers will have bugs. They will have bugs in just about every industry on a daily basis. I have problems with my ATM every once in a while. The airline industry is not perfect. Airplanes don't get to back away on time every single time we take off. Every person in this room has had to shut down their PC and turn it back on again, when it's acting a little strange.

Software has bugs, and, yes, there's no question that as the software gets more complex, there are more lines of code, and a greater probability of discovering a bug. But the answer is not to make the software simpler or to remove it or to slow it down. The answer is to perform better when the events happen. That's something that we, as exchanges, and as the clearing houses, have committed to the SEC to do – to work together to improve our obvious error policies, our halt processes, and in how we shut down the markets, and in how we reopen the markets. Let me say this: We really can do better as an industry. We can work together to try to stop these things from happening. But it's not going to eliminate all of them in the future.

Pisani: Are our expectations too high for technology? At what point did we think it was going to work all the time? I remember when I first came to the stock exchange in '96. The SuperDOT system went down all the time.[31] All the time. It went down so often that I never reported it. I'd walk up to one of the specialists and ask, what's going on? And he'd say, "Oh, the SuperDOT's down." I'd respond with, "Oh, all right." Now, maybe, because the markets are today interconnected so much, we expect them to work perfectly. We're shocked, shocked, that something actually happens, whether it's a line of code, or some other temporary setback.

[31] SuperDot was the electronic system used by the New York Stock Exchange to route market and limit orders from investors, or their agents, to a specialist on the floor of the exchange. SuperDot was the upgraded and predecessor system of the Designated Order Turnaround (DOT) system. In 2009, SuperDOT was replaced by the NYSE Super Display Book system (SDBK) for processing orders. In 2012, the Display Book was replaced by the Universal Trading Platform (UTP).

But let me not let you wiggle out of it that easy. What about the cost of this whole thing? Look, the stock trading business is lousy.[32] These are publicly traded companies. Number one, should they be publicly traded companies? Number two, how do we make sure that people spend enough money so that they actually work? If you're a high-frequency trader, you're in an arms race against other high-frequency traders.

One of the problems they're having right now is that this arms race costs a lot of money. They're not making as much money because the volatility is low. So they're in a bit of trouble. They have to spend or get out. Should exchanges be forced to spend more? Should there be more regulation to that? Should publicly traded exchanges be required to spend more? Should there be more regulation around technology? Reg SCI is sitting out there in front of the SEC.[33] I'll bet you they do nothing with it. I said it right to Dan Gallagher, the commissioner, who was on our air the other day. I asked him, are you going to vote for it? Dan said, "I'm still studying" it. They've been studying it for 3 years. They're not going to do anything. That's my cynical opinion as a reporter.

Katz: Let me give you a good, quick example of the difference between smart regulation and intelligent regulation. The entire options market continued to function. We back each other up. There are 12 different options exchanges. Yet, as part of Reg SCI, the regulator is considering adding an enormous cost onto each of the exchanges – which they each have not just a backup site but, on top of that, they must have a disaster recovery, or DR, site over 300 miles away from their primary and backup site. Do we really need a DR site for each exchange, when each exchange is the DR site for the other exchange? That is intelligent regulation – looking at what we have and rationalizing where we spend our money. That is not to say that we shouldn't have redundancy in the SIP.[34] Because SIP going down should not cause the entire market to stop operating for 3 h.

Pisani: It is extraordinary that the NASDAQ SIP should not be backed up by the NYSE SIP.

---

[32] "Lousy" here is referring to Pisani's later comment that some traders are not making "much money" because market volatility was low at the time of this conference. Higher levels of volatility can drive profitability for traders.

[33] Regulation Systems Compliance and Integrity (Regulation SCI) is a set of rules created by the US Securities and Exchange Commission to monitor the security and capabilities of US securities markets' technological infrastructure. The Commission adopted Regulation SCI and Form SCI in November 2014. Regulation SCI replaced the SEC's Automation Review Policy guidelines, developed in 1989 and 1991 after the 1987 market crash known as Black Monday, when the Dow Jones Industrial Average plummeted 23%.

[34] "The Security Information Processor (SIP) links the US markets by processing and consolidating all protected bid/ask quotes and trades from every trading venue into a single, easily consumed data feed." Source: Consolidated Tape Association.

More broadly, the NYSE and NASDAQ, at time of writing, each operated a SIP for US stock exchanges, the former showing the best bid and offer for NYSE-listed stocks, the latter showing the NBBO for NASDAQ stocks. These data processors consolidate quote and trade data for stocks listed on their exchanges. The data is then disseminated for a fee to investors, market-data providers, and others. NYSE also operated a SIP for options exchanges.

Katz: That is what SEC Chair White has asked the exchanges to look at. There are many times when you say to yourself, why didn't I think of that? Everybody in the room sort of said the SIP had been working all these years, that there has never been an outage. It was not the area that we focused on, and now it's something that we have to focus on. Continuous improvement should be the motto. But we should have a rational expense. We shouldn't just spend money to say that we spent money, if it doesn't add any value and redundancy in the marketplace.

Pisani: Keith, I know you feel that way, too.

Ross: John said it well earlier when he talked about principles-based rules.[35] That's something that's easy to get behind because it makes a lot of sense. As for some of the SCI ideas like cataloging algorithms, I just don't see how it could be effective other than increasing costs for everyone.[36]

Pisani: Can you explain further?

Ross: The algorithms change. Some even change on the fly during the day. So it's not the algorithm that you need to monitor. It's the output of the algorithm. Many years ago when I was with a high-frequency firm, we literally had thousands of models that we changed constantly during the day. Listen to how regulators are talking right now in terms of monitoring algorithms. In my opinion, that approach just would not work.

Let me spend a moment on why maker-taker is so misunderstood. When you post a price, you are opening yourself to adverse selection. When I put my price out, someone can either hit my bid if it's a two-sided market or they can take my offer. When I started earlier in my career with the ECN model, to get dealers, and the high-frequency guys, to put prices up, a rebate had to be paid. Back in those days, the markets were wide enough. Indeed they were multiple cents wide before the introduction of penny pricing. We were talking about Citicorp earlier today being traded at $4. The high-frequency guys today can, in effect, now earn the rebate on both sides of this market today, and the bid-ask spread is effectively a fraction of a penny.

People look at that and they say maker-taker. You're making people pay the money for the liquidity. It is unfair. Well, in fact, it turns out they're going to pay for it anyway![37] They're going to pay for it in some percentage of the bid-ask spread,

[35] See 12.

[36] See 33.

[37] In a follow-up interview, Ross further defended the maker-taker model, saying it was a way to reward participants, market makers, and HFT traders, for posting bids and offer in a marketplace where spreads have narrowed with the aforementioned advent of penny trading. In the past, the spread was wide enough to allow market makers to make money. Ross uses the analogy of the common practice of tipping restaurant staff in America. "In Europe, the tip is included, so adding the tip in the US is closer to the maker taker model," he said. What about reported abuses of the maker taker model, such as rapid-fire trading for rebates? "It occurs in any market anyway, and not because of maker taker. I think it is a confusion of symptom with the problem. And so I discount that idea very heavily," he responded.

because the dealers have to make a little money to be able to continue to make markets. So sometimes when I hear people talk about maker-taker, I think it's not well understood; yet it's actually an incredible efficiency in the marketplace.

Pisani: A lot of people don't look at it that way. But I appreciate the perspective. Does anybody have any questions for the panel?

Steven Saxs [Chief Compliance Officer, FBN Securities]: Today many firms are using OMSs to route their orders to various venues including the exchanges.[38] I know the exchanges seem to have very good controls and firewalls. I've never heard anybody take a stab at who's reviewing these OMSs. Some of them are not regulated. Anybody could work at them; the servers could be anywhere in the world. I've never heard of a server going down or an OMS breaking down. I've heard of exchanges breaking down. Is that an area you think needs some review, since everything now is IT oriented?

Kelly: It so happens that the founder and CEO of Liquidnet, Seth Merrin, is also the inventor of the order management system (OMS). Seth created the first OMS in 1985, as a way to automate paper trade tickets, and the OMS has since become a ubiquitous and essential tool. Traders and portfolio managers can choose from approximately 40 different OMS vendors, to manage and trade their order book.

Since OMS systems have a broad support function, it is important to choose a system that also offers tools to meet internal risk and compliance requirements. Think of an OMS as a communications tool that enables a portfolio manager or trader to send messages for trade interest. However, the trade execution takes place on regulated venues, such as exchanges and alternative trading systems (ATS) like Liquidnet.

Sachs: I'm talking about somebody who actually hacks into the system to see that valuable order flow. People talk about the 40 different OMSs. They see a significant amount of flow, and their servers could be all over the world. The question is about hacking. Has there ever been a case of somebody actually hacking in and seeing if somebody has taken advantage of that order flow?

Kelly: Not to my knowledge. I agree. The buyer of that OMS, of that application, should certainly dive into all of the questions that you've just raised and satisfy themselves.

Pisani: Let me take another question here.

Joe Rosen: I'm not a Luddite. Just because you can do something faster in our markets doesn't mean that it is necessarily a good thing and that you should do it.

---

[38] An OMS is an electronic platform that facilitates and manages the order execution of securities, typically through the FIX protocol. Order management systems are used on both the buy-side and the sell-side.

By way of analogy, perhaps someone who has had a very good year on Wall Street goes out and buys a Maserati that will travel at speeds up to 200 miles an hour. That doesn't mean you should be doing 200 miles an hour down Wall Street.

Ross: Short answer, if you trade more quickly, you take less risk. If you take less risk, you can make better markets. So the reason for the speed is actually to make a better market, because each trade entails less risk and you have a better distribution.

Van Slyke: John Kelly talked earlier about order size tending to drop from year to year. If you do smaller orders you have less risk. And so there's an inevitable progression to faster trading and to smaller orders. The question is, on what kind of platform are you going to do that? We are getting some advice from Bob Schwartz, because we're looking at a pure auction-based system with call auctions running at, perhaps, once a second. The purchases are all disclosed, but the bids are all dark. We think that will drive down the order size and drive up the frequency. We think that is good for price discovery.

Kelly: I am always on guard to not use these forums as an advertising session, but I have to disagree. At Liquidnet, our average trade is 42,000 shares, compared to approximately 250 shares at other trading venues. Our system aggregates all orders and places them in a pool where traders can manually and anonymously negotiate the trade. Our research shows that we have a 90% negotiation success rate, meaning our members are getting more trades done at a price that is cost-effective and with technology that's optimized for efficiency. I understand there is a market for smaller orders. But we're seeing evidence to the contrary on our system.

Van Slyke: At least in your big block trading. For the large blocks, it's so important to treat them differently.

Ross: But you're only dealing with a segment of the market when two naturals come together. Because 97% of the market today is not naturals meeting each other.[39] It's someone wanting liquidity at a specific point in time. That's why the rest of the market is so volatile. It's a great service that you provide, but it's a niche.

Pisani: Here's my final question on high-frequency trading. What if they scalp a penny? I'm turning this upside down, and our viewers will be furious if I even think that I'm approving of them in any way. But suppose Apple is worth $500 a share. Should high-frequency traders have a right to charge a toll? If its $500, and you're buying it for a year, and the effective cost of getting in on that is $500.01, does that matter? Should we care? Should that be a legitimate issue? I'm talking about the toll that it costs.

[39] Referring to block trading where two naturals meet each other.

Ross: The margins are not a penny; they're a 20th of a penny. The margins are incredibly small, about 20% of the rebate for the HFT guys.[40]

Pisani: For me, it will effectively cost $500.01. But I'm asking the question, does that matter?

Ross: I would think not, but I'm not your typical viewer.

Pisani: Anybody else?

Katz: I don't think that it should matter. Most importantly because, if you don't have the high-frequency trader making that fraction of that penny, then we don't have liquidity on the screens, and the customer will not be paying $500.01. They will pay $500.50, because they will only be able to interact with another natural customer. And that's what the data were demonstrating in the material that we saw earlier at this conference today – the high-frequency trader is effectively providing liquidity. I think we will ultimately have to live with the structure that we have today and, in that structure, they are providing the liquidity. I don't think we should assume that it will change tomorrow.

Pisani: Thank you, gentlemen, we appreciate it.

---

[40] Ross explained, in a follow-up, by offering the example of 5 cents profit seemingly made on a 100-share trade by one of these same HFT guys, posting at $500.01, or a penny a share. In reality, this is not 5 cents profit, he argued; rather the profit is a fraction of a penny since the same trader may take losses on as many as half his trades and as adverse selection is subtracted in the calculation.

Chapter 5
A Trader's Perspective

Andrew M. Brooks

When Bob Schwartz asked me to speak here today, he provided me this wonderful bully pulpit, along with his permission to choose any topic under the market structure sun. So I thought about what we struggle with most today. Much of that is part of the overall struggle with market structure and the tension that naturally occurs in markets. Somebody earlier this morning said that markets naturally want to come together and that networks want to come together too. That is true.

One of the takeaways for me today is this: We've put too many obstacles in the way of trading interests coming together. Think about the mandate of the National Market System.[1] It was designed to bring markets closer together, not to put obstacles in their way. Maybe we could work together to remove any obstacles before us. Let me pick up on this theme in a moment.

The more things change, the more they remain the same. Yes, we still struggle with market structure. For some historical perspective, I reached back into the archives. Here's the April 1994 issue of *Traders Magazine,* with a younger version of myself in the cover photo and story. [Brooks holds cover aloft.] I thought to myself, "Okay, the cover says, "Seeking Fair Play in the Equity Traders Ball Game." I reread this article and, lo and behold, so many of the issues are still the same".

---

[1] See the Securities Exchange Act of 1934 and Regulation National Market System (NMS) for context. The Securities Exchange Act of 1934 is the federal legislation launched on June 4, 1975, to amend the Securities Exchange Act of 1934. The 1975 amendments instructed the Securities and Exchange Commission to cooperate with the industry in creating a National Market System along with an ambitious system for the clearance and settlement of securities transactions nationwide. The amendments also provided for the prohibition of fixed-commission rates, promulgated earlier by the SEC in its Rule 19b-3.

Reg NMS (Regulation National Market System) was adopted by the Securities and Exchange Commission in 2005 and introduced 2 years later to further advance the ideals of a national market system. The regulation includes the order protection or trade-through rule, access rule (fair access) to market data including quotations, and rules on sub-penny trading and on market data.

A. M. Brooks (✉)
T. Rowe Price Associates, Inc., Baltimore, MD, USA

© Springer Nature Switzerland AG 2019
R. A. Schwartz et al. (eds.), *Market Integrity*, Zicklin School of Business Financial Markets Series, https://doi.org/10.1007/978-3-030-02871-8_5

Sure, I've aged a bit, but we continue to talk about the same things! And so sometimes we make no progress. As much as they remain the same, other things have changed – speed, electronics, algorithms, all kind of other things have changed. In response, traders and investors have had to adapt new technologies and processes.

I want to accomplish two things today. First, I need 9 min of your time to lay out an agenda for what needs to get done in market structure. That's what Congress should propose too, no more than 9 min to get certain business done, and then move on to the next order of business. Second, I want to take a line from Eric Miller, a former strategist at DLJ.[2] He used to write "Random Gleanings" in their weekly research report. In the spirit of Eric, today I want to give you some of my own random gleanings.

To start, let's talk about 10 things I would change in my 9 min. I am intentionally making this somewhat controversial, perhaps to generate some excitement and some questions.

First, let's abolish the maker-taker model.[3] It seems so perverse to me. Is there any other form of commerce where you can both buy and sell something at the same price and make money doing it? That's pretty much what maker-taker does. It doesn't seem right to me.

Second, let's eliminate payment for order flow.[4] Inducements for order flow must surely interfere with best execution.[5] There is an inherent conflict of interest here. Why are we paying for it?

Third, let's affirm a trade-at rule, which requires meaningful price improvement, half of the spread at a minimum.[6] I don't know what the spread should be. But it can't be, and it should not be, a penny for all stocks. That doesn't seem right to me.

Four, let's reduce fragmentation and complexity. Perhaps a market center with close to de minimis market share should be ignored. We have this obligation to satisfy all quotes to uphold our trade-through obligations and to not trade-through.[7]

---

[2] Donaldson, Lufkin & Jenrette (DLJ) was the US investment bank founded by William H. Donaldson, Richard Jenrette, and Dan Lufkin in 1959 and later acquired by Credit Suisse.

[3] In a competitive program to encourage trading on exchanges, maker-taker fees offer a transaction rebate to trading participants who provide liquidity and a charge to customers who take liquidity.

[4] Compensation and benefit paid to brokerages for sending their orders to different venues for execution.

See Payment for Order Flow. Professionals Pay to Make Trades for Small Investors. Annie Massa, May 20, 2016, Bloomberg. www.bloomberg.com/quicktake/payment-for-order-flow

[5] Under US securities law, brokers are required obtain the best execution reasonably available for customer orders. See Best Execution, www.sec.gov/answers/bestex.htm

[6] At the time of the conference, exchanges had been lobbying the Securities and Exchange Commission to introduce a rule that would force equities transactions onto so-called lit exchanges unless dark pools, or internalizing matching engines, could show that reasonable price improvement had been achieved (unlike the lit markets, dark pools do not display prices to investors).

[7] A trade-through occurs when a stock market order is not executed at the best possible price based on quoted prices at other exchanges. More specifically, the trade-through was enshrined by Securities and Exchange Commission when it enacted Reg NMS (National Market System) in 2005: "A trade-through occurs when one trading center executes an order at a price that is inferior to the price of a protected quotation, often representing an investor limit order, displayed by another trading center," the SEC explained.

But let's face it, a market center with only an insignificant half of 1% in market share can tie me up as a trader. It is not really providing any value when I have an order to complete; it has no depth when it comes to the quote. I'm not sure I should hold our broker responsible and require him to go to that market center. Let's blow right through it. Screw it! You're out. In other words, if you have an insignificant market share, and the only thing you are competing on is the price of executions, it seems to me we ought to be able to opt out and ignore that. I think institutional investors should be able to do that. I wonder if that wouldn't make the market a little bit better. On the other hand, if you bring value as a market center to the marketplace, let's respect that. But if pricing is all you have to offer as a market center, I'm not sure that's enough to qualify you as an exchange today.

Five, let's require that dark pools[8] have a minimum execution size. We heard that discussed a lot today. I am absolutely in favor of that. Dark pools were given a free pass to encourage trading in size. Yet the average size in the dark pools is less than it is on average in the lit markets. That's crazy. That's wrong. That's not what was intended, and we should circle back on that. When dark pools were introduced, the intention was to encourage block trading in minimum trade sizes of 5000–10,000 shares. Yet the exact opposite has happened. So, how perverse is it that we allow for the proliferation of all these dark pools in the hope of trading in size when, in reality, the average trade size is less than it is on the lit exchanges (which is about 180–200 shares) and, by the way, the minimum trade size on the dark pools ought to be 5000 shares, not 500 or 200 shares. I would not make the minimum size as small as that. It should be something that's legitimate and more substantial. We ought to foster transparency in the markets. Frankly, we're not doing that with all those dark pools.

We, on the buy-side, are part of the problem. Because we're sending some of our orders to the dark pools, the buy-side is absolutely complicit in this matter. By the way, we on the buy-side don't have all the answers either. But we are certainly part of the problem!

Six, let's experiment with minimum increments based on trading volumes. The one-size-fits-all approach doesn't work. I'm thinking about penny, 3 cents, 5 cents, and 10 cents increments. And, contrary to the opinion of a lot of very smart people this morning, please do not allow quoting in sub-penny increments. Quoting in sub-pennies is a sub-optimal approach, simply because it will encourage participants to route orders as small as a mere 100 shares in size, for sub-penny price improvement. What does that amount to on 100 shares? There is simply no economic sense in this. It is asinine; it is ridiculous. To say you will route an order based on a sub-penny price improvement is like saying, "I'm sorry, will you even go give me a penny if I trade 100 shares?" Is that the improvement? Let's not go there; we've got better things to do. I just can't honestly see any good coming from that.

[8] See Dark Pools: Fear of the Dark. Third Way. Lauren Oppenheimer, John Valley. August 28, 2013. http://www.thirdway.org/report/dark-pools-fear-of-the-dark

As the authors explain: "Dark pools are private, electronic stock trading venues that allow buyers and sellers of a stock to be matched anonymously. In a dark pool, prices are not displayed to investors—stock prices are dark. Dark trading is an alternative to trading on a 'lit' exchange, like the New York Stock Exchange (NYSE), where traders benefit from visible prices."

Seven, demand the introduction of the consolidated audit trail, as soon as possible, to monitor the life cycle of a trade.[9] We can't wait much longer. What is that about? How many billions is it supposed to cost, $4 billion?

Voice [From the audience]: Less than that.

Brooks: Less than that. Well, it's a big number, and yet some people in the industry say it can be built in about 6 months and at a cost of say, $100 million. Let's engage those people. We still haven't learned from Long-Term Capital.[10] We still don't know who's on the other side of trades today. We don't know who's doing what. How crazy is that? This is a little frustrating; it should be something that regulators at a very high level can address. They should know everybody who is involved in everything. Especially when you're talking about the national interest.

Eight, let's think about establishing a minimum quote-to-trade ratio. Some forms of high-frequency trading are terrific, I'm sure. But other forms of HFT strategies, say entering and cancelling orders 98 out of 100 times when buying 100 shares of, say, GE, are certainly questionable. Now I'm not sure why exactly they're really doing this, but it sounds awfully manipulative to me. It sounds disingenuous; it does not sound constructive. It does not sound like high-frequency trading is constructively adding to the market structure. That should be something to look at. And, by the way, what a perfect thing to experiment with. I don't know what the quote-to-trade ratio should be, say one out of 20 times – 20:1 – you pick the number, but let's try it. If your only strategy is to slow the marketplace down so that you can manipulate it, jam it with data, congest the system, clog the pipe – pick your analogy – I say pick up your marbles, and go somewhere else. This behavior sounds bad to me.

Nine, let's do an exhaustive audit of order routing practices. Wouldn't that be refreshing? Where are you sending your orders? How come? What are you doing it for? What are you gaining? What advantage are you looking for? And, in this way, wouldn't we be affirming the sanctity of the national best bid and offer?[11]

---

[9] The Consolidated Audit Trail, aimed at tracking the life cycle of all stock and options orders, was approved by the Securities and Exchange Commission on November 15, 2016, a system with a reported price tag of $2.4 billion.

See *SEC Approves Plan to Create Consolidated Audit Trail.* https://www.sec.gov/news/press-release/2016-240.html.

SEC Approves Consolidated Audit Trail to Detect Market Manipulation. Audit trail to track life cycle of every trade in U.S. market. David Michaels, Wall Street Journal, November 15, 2016. http://www.wsj.com/articles/sec-to-vote-on-consolidated-audit-trail-to-detect-market-manipulation-1479240411

[10] Long-Term Capital Management L.P. was a hedge fund management firm in Greenwich, CT., employing absolute-return trading strategies along with high financial leverage. The firm's Long-Term Capital Portfolio L.P. collapsed in the late 1990s and was bailed out in 1998 under Federal Reserve Supervision.

[11] The NBBO, National Best Bid and Offer. In simple terms, the National Best Bid and Offer requires brokers under US regulation to guarantee that customers receive the best prevailing ask price when they buy securities and the best prevailing bid price when they sell.

The Code of Federal Regulations explains: "National best bid and national best offer means, with respect to quotations for an NMS Security, the best bid and best offer for such security that are calculated and disseminated on a current and continuing basis by a plan processor pursuant to an effective national market system plan."

I've heard this posited in a number of different ways. But this is the question, as I would ask it: Can we please ask for a comparison of the time stamps from direct feeds versus the Securities Industry Processor (or SIP) for every single quote and every single trade?[12] And, can we do it for a random period, say every other day for a month? That is to say, can we examine each direct fee quote matched up with the quote from the SIP? What is the difference between the time stamps? Might we discover that we're violating Reg NMS or certainly the spirit of a national market system?[13]

With the trading markets moving as fast as they are today, I'm not sure the NBBO has any real value.[14] What does it mean if a market participant knows the NBBO is actually going to change and they trade on that change? Does the NBBO have any real meaning when there is all this high-speed trading activity going on around it? If you have market participants engaged in arbitrage, profiting from the slight time difference between the direct feed and the SIP feed, does the NBBO have any value in these instances? What does it mean if someone already knows the NBBO is going to change and this person trades on that change versus the NBBO? It flies in face of the requirement of Reg NMS. MIDAS[15] and some of these other systems out there might be able to present us with the related facts on this. Are we respecting the NBBO? Isn't that a requirement of Reg NMS?

---

[12] Larry Tabb, writing in the Tabb Forum in December 2016, notes the concept of the consolidated/aggregated market data feed in the US equities markets.

Tabb explains: "Data for the consolidated feed is published by the various exchanges, aggregated by the Securities Information Processors (SIPs), and then distributed to the SIPs' subscribers (either directly or through market data providers). The consolidated feeds historically are slower than exchange direct feeds. While the SIPs have been working on accelerating aggregated data feeds, the process of significantly improving SIP latencies and robustness shifted into overdrive after the August 2013 SIP outage that closed the US equity markets for 3 h. Many market participants believe that if we can reduce SIP latency, it will reduce latency arbitrage and create a fairer and more efficient market. While this is true, eliminating direct feed/SIP latency arbitrage is more complicated than just speeding up the SIP."

SIP defined: "The Security Information Processor (SIP) links the US markets by processing and consolidating all protected bid/ask quotes and trades from every trading venue into a single, easily consumed data feed." Source: Consolidated Tape Association.

More broadly, the NYSE and NASDAQ, at time of writing, each operated a SIP for US stock exchanges, the former showing the best bid and offer for NYSE-listed stocks and the latter showing the NBBO for NASDAQ stocks. These data processors consolidate quote and trade data for stocks listed on their exchanges. The data is then disseminated for a fee to investors, market-data providers, and others. NYSE also operated a SIP for options exchanges.

[13] Reg NMS (Regulation National Market System) was adopted by the Securities and Exchange Commission in 2005 and introduced 2 years later to further advance the ideals of a national market system. The regulation includes the order protection or trade-through rule, access rule (fair access) to market data including quotations, and rules on sub-penny trading and on market data.

[14] See 11.

[15] Earlier in 2013, the Securities and Exchange Commission launched its internal Market Information Data Analytics System (MIDAS), which provides the agency with data about every displayed order posted on national exchanges. According to the SEC, MIDAS collects one billion records time-stamped to the microsecond. "The information comes from the consolidated tapes and proprietary feeds of each exchange and includes posted orders and quotes, modifications and cancellations, and trade executions both on- and off-exchange," the SEC notes.

Number 10. We should reestablish clear lines of demarcation between brokers and exchanges. What exactly separates brokers from exchanges today? What can exchanges legally do in quoting and trading activities, compared to brokers in these same areas? Some overlap in these areas between exchanges and brokers today may not be such a good thing. Think back to when, in the past, this kind of overlap did not exist. Wouldn't that change be refreshing? I'm not sure who is who today. Boy, things are pretty cloudy. At some point I wonder if we wouldn't be better off by putting Glass-Steagall[16] back in place. From a globally competitive perspective, maybe that would be a challenge. But it might be terrific from another perspective.

Here are some random gleanings of my own. Our insatiable quest for microsecond and millisecond trading speeds is supersonic speed. It weakens the very foundation of our marketplace. To promote rapid-fire trading often sacrifices redundancy and reliability and that, in turn, can lead to system-wide instability. I'm no technologist. But the experts I talk to say that every time you remove a redundancy in the quest for speed, it's like taking a 2 × 4 out from under the playroom. You're just weakening things. And we've had all these crazy systems outages in our marketplace.[17]

It was a great discussion here earlier today about SuperDOT[18] led by Bob Pisani of CNBC. Remember when SuperDOT went down all the time? Boy, we're moving a lot faster today than we did back in the days of SuperDOT. There's a lot more going on now; and we've had these systems outages too. That undermines investor confidence. Which, of course, also means you've all these people invested in money market funds today, earning 0% interest, when the stock market is up 17% so far this year. That's a lot of people to feel sorry for. I don't know why more investors are not invested in the market. Maybe we've done a lousy job as investment managers trying to encourage investing that it seems to me the quest for high-speed trading is, in any event, a problem. Speed for its own sake should not be the Holy Grail nor the singular pursuit of the industry.[19]

---

[16] The Glass-Steagall Act, also formally known as the Banking Act of 1933, was passed in 1933 by Congress in 1933, as an emergency response to the collapse of some 5000 banks during the Great Depression. The law, repealed in 1999, was designed to prohibit commercial banks from engaging in the investment business and establishing a division between both sides of the banking business.

[17] Aside from flash crashes, there were well-reported glitches. For example, the price of the stock in Kraft Foods (NASDAQ: KRFT) surged 25% within 1 min soon after the market opened. This glitch was blamed on a broker error by NASDAQ that affected multiple exchanges. "Investors were hit with another stock-trading glitch Wednesday, this one in a household name – Kraft Foods – which saw dozens of trades canceled when a broker error caused shares to soar shortly after the opening bell," according to *The Wall Street Journal*. See Kraft Hit by Trading Glitch, *Wall Street Journal,* October 3, 2012, Alexandra Scaggs and Matt Jarzemsky.

[18] The electronic system of the New York Stock Exchange once used to route market and limit orders from customers, or their agents, to a specialist on the floor of the exchange. SuperDOT succeeded the Designated Order Turnaround (DOT) system. By 2009, SuperDOT was replaced by the NYSE's Super Display Book system.

[19] For additional information, see Robert A. Schwartz and Liuren Wu, "Equity Trading in the Fast Lane: The Staccato Alternative," The Journal of Portfolio Management Invited Editorial, Spring 2013, 39 (3) 3–6; DOI: https://doi.org/10.3905/jpm.2013.39.003. (Reprinted in this book on page 97).

Is anyone responsible for the quote anymore? Does anybody care about the quote? Should anybody care? Should someone be able to raise their hand and say, "You know what, there's a problem in this stock." I think I have to halt it. Back in the day, the specialist and market maker were responsible for the quote. Who validates the quote today?

And that reminds me: The speaker this morning from the CBOE talked about 15,000 orders coming in from 1 customer alone. He then wanted to call his competitor, to see if he was also seeing these orders. I really wanted to ask the speaker, did you call the customer and ask, "Hey, man, what are you doing, what's going on with these orders? Why are you sending me 15,000 orders?" By the same token, somebody today needs to be responsible for the quote, which is the basis for which we make all our decisions. Look, we are overly complex in our approach to market structure. I don't exactly know why. We have some 10 stock exchanges and 50-plus dark pools.[20] We are too complex. Can we please experiment with pilot programs so we can figure this all out?

I was telling somebody over lunch that we're in the batting average game. If I bat 550, I'm absolutely in the hall of fame. I'm from Baltimore, so I'm a major Orioles fan; we didn't make it this year, too bad! But it seems as if our regulators and others are very hesitant, reluctant, or intransigent, to encourage and to adopt pilot programs, to learn from what we're doing right or wrong.

Every academician I've ever met has a thirst for data. I want data too. Here's an opportunity to generate your own data, clean data, Bob [Schwartz]; do it. Whatever you want. Let's get the data and give academicians a further chance to examine more things about our markets. We make mistakes all the time. I have to raise my hand and say, I have made a mistake. Washington, you guys don't make mistakes? Of course, we all make mistakes! Everybody does. It would be refreshing to hear regulators say we have strayed from the spirit of the National Market System of 1975.[21] Perhaps we need to revisit and rethink Reg NMS.[22] The SEC seems hesitant to admit it went too far in this regard. We all make mistakes from time to time. Investment managers can make mistakes. So in that light, a bit of humility is needed from the regulators. Why don't we experiment in an effort to get things right? Maybe with a new sheriff, Mary Jo White,[23] coming to town, we can perhaps get some pilot programs launched on various aspects of our market structure; so in that way we can learn from our experience and try then to do better.

---

[20] See 8. Two years later, *Reuters* reported that the USA supported 11 stock exchanges.

[21] Refers to federal legislation introduced on June 4, 1975, to amend the Securities Exchange Act of 1934. The 1975 amendments instructed the Securities and Exchange Commission to cooperate with the industry in creating a National Market System, along with an ambitious system for the clearance and settlement of securities transactions nationwide. The amendments also provided for the prohibition of fixed-commission rates, promulgated earlier by the SEC in its Rule 19b-3.

[22] See 13.

[23] Mary Jo White was sworn in the 31st Chair of the Securities and Exchange Commission on April 10, 2013, and as of writing was stepping down in January 2017.

Here's another thing: Companies ought to split their stock. You know, everybody is trying to be the next Warren Buffett. Warren Buffett must surely be a terrific investor, but gee whiz, he's made mistakes, and he never splits his company stock, Berkshire Hatheway. Look at the size of these company shares as another example: Price line is at $900 and change; Mastercard is over $500. The average stock price used to be $25 to $30; now it's about $67 or $68 a share. We need a healthy ecosystem. Inordinately high prices don't cut it.[24]

People push back and say, if you split your stock, you've got to pay more in commissions. You're right. But do you want a healthy ecosystem? I do. And I am willing to say, I'll pay a little more to make sure that the community is safe, that the community is vibrant, that the community is healthy. Yes, I think that's a good thing to do. I would urge all of you to encourage the companies you work for or others to say, "Hey, man, think about splitting your stock. I don't see a downside from that, I really don't. And, by the way, our model is not built on volume, but still we need more volume in the system."[25]

Can we look at this insidious business of aggregating and selling investors' data? Everybody is repackaging the trade data, the quote data, all that stuff. But it's the investors' data they're repackaging and selling. And, by the way, the people who want to buy it are paying a lot of money for it.[26] Back in the 1990s, I was on an SEC advisory committee on market data that was assembled by Arthur Levitt, then Chairman of the SEC. Selling data then was a $500 million business. Today, it has been repackaged into, I'm guessing, a multi-billion dollar business.[27]

But so much of this quest for the data is ultimately about people trying to figure out our trading interests: what we on the buy-side are buying and selling on behalf of our clients. We view that as material nonpublic information. You do not have a right to know that. You should not be engaged in a commercial enterprise, trying to find out what we're trading.

In this regard, I must point out that companies today, under SEC law, can request information on the aggregate change of holdings of a security at custodians and broker dealers. They can obtain that within 4 or 5 days after the trade date. So, people can obtain and analyze data on the changes in ownership of a security. In this

---

[24] High stock prices are still an issue in the aftermath of the conference. See CEO sounds of on Wall Street's high share prices, John Aidan Byrne. *New York Post*, June 11, 2016 http://nypost.com/2016/06/11/bats-ceo-sounds-off-on-wall-streets-high-share-price

[25] Ibid.

[26] Trading data continued to be an increasingly controversial topic in the industry in the wake of this conference, with critics complaining about rising costs. As an example of the costs charged data users, Intercontinental Exchange, which owns NYSE, data, and connectivity sales were $477 m, or 41%, of revenues in the first quarter of 2016. That was up 6% for the year, and data sales alone rose 9% annually.

See *There's a new 'hot-button' issue on Wall Street, and battle lines are being drawn. BusinessInsider*, Matt Turner, November 3, 2016 http://www.businessinsider.com/stock-exchanges-market-data-cost-becoming-big-issue-2016-10 Matt Turner, November 3, 2016.

Fight Over Market Data Fees Is Going to Get Ugly, TabbForum, Larry Tabb. December 28, 2016 http://tabbforum.com/opinions/fight-over-market-data-fees-is-going-to-get-ugly

[27] Ibid.

way, market surveillance firms (let's call them) can make informed assessments of who has bought and sold stock, and they can then sell that information to market participants. This practice is happening before any filing is made.

My point here is that people are figuring out information about who is trading what, and that's not right. That's not fair. Issuers don't need to know who is buying and selling their stock so frequently. People who want that information are trying to take advantage at the expense of our clients. We absolutely believe, as investment managers, that that's not right. Perhaps it's someone trying to estimate, guess or reverse engineer, or put together the mosaic, to find out who is trading what.

Markets open at 9:30 AM, and they close at 4:00 PM. Trades settle, and things work pretty well. The retail investor seemingly has the best possible deal going in the world, at about $7.95 a trade, and instantaneous executions. Yet, that trade is really not $7.95 at Charles Schwab or Scottrade, where order flow gets sold and stocks are bought on margin.[28] The discount brokers benefit from the customer margin account balances. In other words, there's a lot going on here that augments that $7.95. That adds on an extra cost to that same payment, and the client doesn't know about it. Let's have some transparency in this arrangement. Maybe that trade should be priced at more than $7.95, to reflect the true costs. There seems to be a lot taking place in the background people aren't aware of.

At the end of the day, things have worked pretty well though. Now people have asked, are we better off today than we were 34 years ago when I started in this business? Probably is the answer. But we're still struggling with a lot of things that ought to be addressed. We're doing okay, but we could be doing much better. That's why we're all here today. We're here to look at ways to do better as an industry, for our clients and for our customers. And that's it from the bully pulpit. Questions?

Male voice: Should the exchanges be for profit?

Brooks: I don't work at the SEC, so I'll give you my own opinion. Exchanges could be for profit, but they probably need to be more in the mode of a public utility. The electric utility, the gas transmission company, for example. Exchanges are now doing lots of things to try and generate volume and profitability that could position them to compete with broker dealers, and that might compete with us. I don't think it was the best change.

I remember asking that same question, when there was consolidation of the specialist firms. These firms were being sold for lots of money, for millions and millions of dollars. So I said, "I'm sorry, who owns the company listings? Why is somebody getting paid for this deal?" Before it became a publicly listed company, the New York Stock Exchange was a mutual organization, owned by seat holders, and the value of the exchange was in the listing business of public companies on the exchange.[29] So should an exchange be run more in the mode of a public utility and not as a for-profit exchange?

---

[28] See 4.

[29] The New York Exchange Stock demutualized in 2006 and became a for-profit, publicly traded company.

I don't think the current structure is the best model. I'm very interested in watching Jeffrey Sprecher and his plans for the NYSE.[30] He has done a marvelous job at the helm at ICE. You know, he's certainly been a disrupter. It will be fascinating to watch what he does with this entity, the NYSE that might be a market ripe for change and change that's better for everybody. So let's keep our fingers crossed there.

Male voice: First of all, thank you for your candor, I mean a breath of fresh air. You and I agreed on a lot, so that's good. We hear terms like gaming and predatory trading. Where is the line between predatory trading and gaming versus market manipulation and fraud, number one?[31] And you've been 34 years in this business. However you're defining the real bad stuff, how much of it is going on? On the one hand, you're a trader, so you want to get a good trade done. But one man's manipulative, predatory trade, is another one's good trade, sort of.

Brooks: This struggle is present since at least the Buttonwood Agreement, to be sure, indeed from the beginning of time.[32] And I guess as a buy-side trader myself, we're naturally paranoid. We want our cake, and we want to eat it as well. But our job is to keep the cards held in pretty close and to hire agents who will do the same to protect our trading interests.

It seems like things are out of balance. It seems like we've favored those with the shortest-term investment horizons, the high-frequency style of traders, at the expense of those ordinary retail investors who buy mutual funds and the like and have the longest-term investment horizons. I'm not saying we're more legitimate or have more of a claim. But I think we're out of balance.

I certainly agree with an earlier comment that there are always a few black sheep, that there are always people cheating on their taxes. But most people are doing the right thing. Most people are trying to trade in a reasonable manner. Indeed, talking about time horizon, the average holding period at T. Rowe Price or, for that matter, the average long-term holding period on the buy-side is 2.5–3 years.

I once spoke at the Wharton School at Penn.[33] One of the students asked me why does all this matter, if you guys on the buy-side are long-term investors? Why do

---

[30] Founder, Chairman and CEO of Intercontinental Exchange (ICE) and Chairman of the New York Stock Exchange. ICE acquired the NYSE in 2013. See Buying the N.Y.S.E., in One Shot. New York Times. Nathaniel Popperjan, January 19, 2013 http://www.nytimes.com/2013/01/20/business/jeffrey-sprechers-improbable-path-to-buying-the-nyse.html

[31] See Brooks' earlier comments on his proposal for a quote-to-trade ratio. Related terms (and of a controversial nature) include spoofing and quote stuffing. The latter is the practice of submitting an excessive amount of larger orders to buy or sell stocks in fractions of a second and then cancelling the orders almost immediately.

[32] The Buttonwood Agreement, signed by 24 stock brokers under a buttonwood tree outside of 68 Wall Street, in lower Manhattan, on May 17, 1792, created the New York Stock & Exchange Board, now known as the New York Stock Exchange.

[33] The Wharton School of the University of Pennsylvania is the business school of the University of Pennsylvania, a private university in Philadelphia, Pennsylvania.

you on the buy-side care that somebody is doing something you consider inappropriate? He didn't really understand what was going on. I replied that it's death by 1000 cuts. If somebody is stealing from me, I am still irritated, even if I can amortize that theft over 3 or 10 years; whatever the holding period is, I think it does matter.

And, by the way, just for context, I was startled back in 2007 by that intellectual theft trial in Chicago that impacted Goldman's computer code.[34] Citadel, taking the stand, admitted it had made in excess of a billion dollars in high-frequency trading the previous year. I thought, wow, that's a lot of money. And I'm sure they earned all of it. But, regardless, that's a lot of money from those strategies.

Andrew Upward [Rosenblatt Securities]: Back in 2004 and even earlier, as Reg NMS[35] was being considered and constructed, there was much debate about an opt-out clause for institutional investors with the order protection rule within this regulation. This would have enabled them to essentially pick their price if they wanted to trade a block. Did that always exist? You could always do that, right?

Brooks: Right.

Upward: Were you in favor of that opt-out clause at the time; and do you feel as though restoring an opt-out clause for the order-protection rule would see a lot of the problems go away in today's marketplace?

Brooks: In this regard, if you trade off board and do other things, there are mechanisms that you can employ, and Reg T[36] is one of them.

Let me add that block-size trading interest among professional investors has to be accommodated, as part of a vibrant market structure. In a liquid, or on a lit displayed market,[37] you have to have some rules about protecting the book. Why we don't protect the entirety of the book that's displayed is probably a reasonable question. But in terms of what you are going to print, all the displayed liquidity in pursuit of this goal, up and down the book, should be protected.

Male voice: You mentioned that the vast majority of HFT trades get cancelled before they go through.

Brooks: My understanding is that some HFT strategies employ that kind of technique.

[34] Sergey Aleynikov, the former Goldman Sachs programmer, was accused of stealing the bank's high-frequency trading code.

[35] See 13.

[36] See Regulation T Filings, http://www.finra.org/industry/regulation-t-filings. Source: FINRA.

[37] See 8.

Male voice: Right. And you think that's a deliberate action? Do you think there is something that can be done to deter traders out there from doing that?

Brooks: Yes. If you charged them for this behavior and explained, "Hey, if you are going to have a certain quote rate, or quote-to-trade ratio, which shows a pattern of excessive quotes, you will get charged." That would help deter a questionable pattern of excessive quotes, with minimum trades and excessive cancellation rates. This would be a positive measure.

About a year ago, we did this experiment at T. Rowe Price. We had 2.5 million shares of stock to buy for a pretty liquid stock. Call it Intel, Microsoft, or some stock like that. We utilized a reputable broker dealer's algorithms. Yet, it was represented in the market as 750 million shares before we got these 2.5 million shares of stock filled and completed. So that was a ratio of 300:1, in terms of the overall shares and the original order. 300:1! Let me explain: With this 2.5 million share order to buy, we went into 1000 venues every 14 s, with individual orders of 100 and 200 shares each; and we ultimately represented 750 million shares to the market when it was all totaled up.

Does that sound productive to you when we had only 2.5 million shares to buy? It doesn't to me. And yet that's where we are at. We're using all these systems, because we're hiding our trading interests. We're trying not to disclose our trading interest; and we're going to all these dark pools and to all these other places, to fill large orders. It's dysfunctional.

Jim Ross: Andy, we also owe you a debt of gratitude, as well. You've been doing this for decades, and you've always been a leader from the buy-side, giving your honest and sage opinion. I hope more institutional head traders, and buy-side traders in general, take your lead. I also hope they listen to what you're saying and start to share a bit more of their insights.

I want to ask you about post-trade transparency. I know you are very sensitive about your order information. I totally get that and your concerns about people, reverse engineering, and all that stuff. But one of the hallmarks of the dark pool movement, starting in the 1980s, was the idea of pre-trade order transparency. The idea of post-trade transparency came to the fore much later. It has become very much a protected vessel of today's trading. What are your thoughts in light of the recent FINRA proposals for more post-trade data?[38]

Brooks: You mean who would have to advertise their trades or acknowledge their trading interest?

---

[38] See *FINRA Makes Dark Pool Data Available Free to the Investing Public*.

FINRA News Release, June 2, 2014 http://www.finra.org/newsroom/2014/finra-makes-dark-pool-data-available-free-investing-public.

See also ***FINRA Publishes ATS Block-Size Trade Data***, FINRA News Release, October, 3, 2016 http://www.finra.org/newsroom/2016/finra-publishes-ats-block-size-trade-data.

Ross: FINRA is proposing that dark pools will have to make more data publicly available.

Brooks: I don't know if we have a real strong view at T. Rowe Price about this. But, we generally do not like to have our trading advertised if it is being done in a dark pool. We've gone there to be dark, so why would you advertise your order? So, we ask the brokers, the operators of those dark pools, not to advertise our flow and to protect our trading interests. Of course, sometimes we do want the broker to advertise our trading interest. But if we are working our order in a dark pool, that is another matter. We may not want out interest made public.

This is one of those areas where some of us are being duplicitous. We've got to be careful, because we clamor for transparency and yet we want to be able to hide too. There are times when you need to hide; there are times when you're still engaged in a buying or selling program and you'd really rather not have people know where you are. But let's not kid ourselves. Every time a trade hits the tape, there is some information out there as a result. I would urge caution in trying to figure out what the market is entitled to and what the participant needs are for protection. If you're at risk, or you're still buying and selling, it seems to me you have a right to be protected.

As an aside, the buy-side probably gets a D minus for effectiveness, in terms of the market structure dialog. Just like every other entity in the market, it's hard for us to find consensus. I always kid with people, and somebody might cringe at this. I'm fairly certain the person lobbying the SEC the most during the previous decade, say 2000–2010, was none other than Bernie Madoff.[39] When you think about who gets the airtime, the buy-side has been miserable here. We really should try to do a better job to encourage fairness and advocate for our clients.

Right next to the buy-side are the issuers. They haven't done much either. I'm not sure what they're getting for their listing fees. If I was Accenture, where my stock went from $42 down to a penny, or anybody whose stock has been disintermediated like that, I would be apoplectic.[40] I'd probably drag every person I had in the C-suite crowd – from the CEOs to the chief operating officers – with me somewhere, to say you need to fix this. So maybe we can make some progress.

Robert Schwartz: I'm always focusing on price discovery, could you say a word from your perspective as a buy-side guy on the integrity, not of price discovery at this time, but of quantity discovery?

Brooks: Our view at T. Rowe Price is that there is a huge difference between volume and liquidity. And so quantity discovery, or volume discovery, as it is also

[39] Founder of Bernard L. Madoff Investment Securities, better known publicly for perpetrating what is regarded as the largest Ponzi scheme in financial history. Madoff, a former NASDAQ Chairman, was also a market structure activist in Washington, long before this Ponzi scandal was exposed.

[40] *Accenture: Went to a Penny at 2:48 p.m.* Matt Phillips, *Wall Street Journal*, *Marketbeat*, May 6, 2016 http://blogs.wsj.com/marketbeat/2010/05/06/accenture-went-to-a-penny-at-248-pm/

called, are really important to what we do. And the opening and the close, of course, usually experience the biggest prints of the day. In fact, a huge challenge for us, with market structure and fragmentation as it is today, is trying to match up outsized trading interest. We like to say it's important for us to present our portfolio managers' with options when we are in pursuit of this goal.

Here's something you can do today. Assume somebody wants to buy your entire position if you'd like to sell it. Maybe you don't want to sell it; but somebody wants to buy it, so you should be aware of that. Because there's a liquidity opportunity, the markets focus on that, but do so, intermittently. We could probably all do a better job of reaffirming the importance of volume, in the quantity discovery process, because price without quantity really doesn't mean anything. And as for the 100-share quote, I could care less about that.

I think almost all of us should acknowledge that maximizing the confluence of buyers and sellers brings out the best in markets, and that's something we ought to commit to. I believe that's what the National Market System and a bunch of other mandates were looking to achieve.[41] Boy, have we forgotten about that stuff.

Let me conclude by saying I am delighted to be speaking to you today. The challenge to make our markets better never ends. We, as dedicated industry practitioners, continue to strive to make everything work better. Isn't that what the American spirit is all about, trying to make everything better for everyone? A superb conference, like this at Baruch College, presents us all a clear opportunity to do just that and to make our voices heard loudly and clearly. Thank you.

[41] See 1.

Chapter 6
Integrity of Market Regulation

Ken Lehn, Eric Budish, Deanna Dobrowsky, Tom Gira, Eric Swanson, and Steve Wunsch

Ken Lehn: We have a great divergence of fascinating views on this panel and, I must add, from a variety of organizations in the financial services sector. As you know, the SEC published a Concept Release which is a part of the agency's review of the existing structure of securities markets.[1] In tandem with this initiative, the SEC raised this question: Is market regulation keeping pace with changes in technology and trading practices? High-frequency trading (HFT) is one of the areas it specifically singled out. The SEC asked for comments on whether high-frequency trading is a problem. And the agency, having identified some problems, asked if a new set of regulatory initiatives is required.

So, I'll begin by asking the panelists, is high-frequency trading helping or harming market quality? Two, if it is harming market quality, what is the root cause? And three, what, if anything, should regulators do about it?

[1] See Concept Release on Equity Market Structure, January 14, 2010: https://www.sec.gov/rules/concept/conceptarchive/conceptarch2010.shtml

See also SEC Press Release, announcing Concept Release, January 13, 2010: https://www.sec.gov/news/press/2010/2010-8.htm

K. Lehn (✉)
Katz Graduate School of Business, University of Pittsburgh, Pittsburgh, PA, USA

E. Budish
Booth School of Business – University of Chicago, Chicago, IL, USA

D. Dobrowsky
IIROC, Toronto, Canada

T. Gira
FINRA, Washington, DC, USA

E. Swanson
BATS Global Markets, Inc., Lenexa, KS, USA

S. Wunsch
Wunsch Auction Associates, LLC, New York, NY, USA

© Springer Nature Switzerland AG 2019
R. A. Schwartz et al. (eds.), *Market Integrity*, Zicklin School of Business Financial Markets Series, https://doi.org/10.1007/978-3-030-02871-8_6

Eric Budish: We can distinguish between two functions that high-frequency trading firms are performing: one is positive; the other is quite negative. The positive function is the use of sophisticated information technology to perform the functions of liquidity provision and price discovery.

But the second function, which I believe is negative, is that high-frequency trading firms are also engaged in what I think of as sniping or picking off liquidity providers. Say there's a news event that affects prices. Think back, for instance, a couple of weeks ago when the Fed announced it would continue bond buying at its current levels. Or think about any time one price changes in any one market.[2] This has implications for prices in other markets, and it triggers a race amongst high-frequency trading firms as they react to that news. Part of that reaction is a race to pick off liquidity providers.[3]

Consider this: You have some high-frequency trading firms with liquidity providing bids and offers to buy or to sell in the limit order book. Then a news event causes those prices to become stale. There's also a race between HFT firms that are providing liquidity that are doing the good work of providing bids and asks for the market and other HFT firms that, at the same time, are trying to pick off what is now stale liquidity. And that same race, that second negative function performed by HFT firms, ultimately manifests itself in an increased cost of liquidity provision. That then harms the integrity and quality of the market.

So my answer is nuanced, because one part of what high-frequency trading firms are doing is remarkable and very valuable. Any comparison between today's market structure and the market structure of 20 years ago suggests that today's markets are much better for retail and institutional investors. But there is also an associated downside, and that's a negative thing.

Eric Swanson: We look at the market for a sense of who is trading. We've examined our market for a sense of the profile of the brokers trading on the market, and of whether they are HFT participants or not.[4] And the definition of HFT must be broader than what is applied when we look at our market.[5] Most of the activity we see in our market from the various participants has one or more of the characteristics of HFT. Regarding HFT, we are thinking of opportunistic proprietary trading that uses high-speed tools to connect. When we divide it up into the different categories of market participants, the vast majority we see as HFT is really on the liquidity provision side that is on the market makers side. No question, that's the most significant segment in our market. The rest would be traditional bulge-bracket

[2] Referring to the US Federal Reserve's so-called quantitative easing program in the wake of the 2007–2008 financial crisis.

[3] See Quarterly Journal of Economics, Vol. 130 November 2015 Issue 4: The High-Frequency Trading Arms Race: Frequent Batch Auctions as a Market Design Response. Budish, Eric, Peter Cramton, Shim, John. http://faculty.chicagobooth.edu/eric.budish/research/HFT-FrequentBatchAuctions.pdf

[4] For clarity, the speaker was also referring to present practices, insofar as BATS would presumably examine the profile of these brokers as a business practice anyway.

[5] See Chap. 4, Integrity of a Marketplace, for discussion on HFT.

broker dealers. And the slice of HFT that you would think about as kind of proprietary, directional – such as hedge funds – that possibly has some elements of this gaming predatory activity, is a relatively small fraction of the market overall. Under 10% would be from firms that are strictly engaged in proprietary trading.

Budish: We've looked at millisecond-level data from the New York Stock Exchange and from the Chicago Mercantile Exchange.[6] We can look at exactly this kind of picking-off activity.[7] So just to reiterate, what I mean by picking off is that something public happens, say the price in Chicago for the S&P 500 future jumps, that then causes the price in New York for the S&P 500 ETF to become stale. Then, two things ought to happen: One, the prices in New York should adjust, and that's price discovery in action; but the second thing is that other high-frequency trading firms should race to try to exploit the now stale quotes in the ETFs in New York, before the liquidity providers in New York can adjust. All these guys have access to the same technology and to the same cables. It's a very simple trading algorithm. Invariably, liquidity providers sometimes lose that race.

Our research suggests that in that one trade alone – the ES-SPY arbitrage, where ES is the S&P 500 E-Mini Futures contract and SPY is the largest S&P 500 Exchange Traded Fund – there's $75 million a year in arbitrage profits to be earned from exploiting stale quotes.

And that's just one example of a pair of highly correlated securities. Of course, the market abounds with highly correlated securities pairs and public news announcements, like the Fed example from a couple of weeks ago.

We agree a large function that algorithmic trading firms are performing is liquidity provision and price discovery. But there's also this dark side, this negative side if you will. I don't mean it in a judgmental way. It's an optimal, self-interested response to market rules. But I think we have the wrong market rules. Our research suggests that the source of the speed race, of this picking-off activity, this race to be milliseconds faster than the competition – now microseconds faster than the competition – is a testament to something.[8]

Look around the room. Many of you know what a picosecond is, that is, one trillionth of a second. I bet many of you also know the speed of light travel time between New York and Chicago. That is also a testament to something.[9] And my research suggests we should move from a continuous time market, a market in which you can trade literally on the instant, to a market based on discrete time, but very frequent discrete time at that.[10] We're talking about markets that clear once per

[6] Ibid.

[7] Ibid.

[8] Ibid.

[9] According to scientists, it takes light 13.3 milliseconds to travel from Chicago to New York and back again.

[10] In a discrete time model, the system is characterized by a market based on fixed time intervals at a finite rate of change at each interval, rather than the "continuous" time model with almost instant executions as described by the speaker.

second or once per hundred milliseconds. That preserves the beneficial function of algorithmic trading firms which is liquidity and price discovery while eliminating the dark side.

Swanson: Is it really a dark side, or is it more of a gray side? Because, I mean, you're accelerating an efficiency in the market, too, by driving the prices to their fair value, are you not?

Budish: I agree you're driving your prices to their fair value; that's beneficial. But you're doing so at the expense of liquidity providers. In a competitive market, liquidity providers will pass along that expense to investors in the form, our research suggests, of wider than necessary bid-ask spreads or, perhaps more saliently, thinner than necessary markets. Because if you provide a deep market on a continuous limit order book on lit exchanges, any time anything public happens, you will get picked off. Or you're at risk of being picked off for all of the liquidity you have provided.[11] It's a technical form of adverse selection at very high-frequency time intervals.

Swanson: At the end of the day, I don't know if your solution really creates more efficiency and better pricing mechanisms. Because you're going to have wider spreads if you go to noncontinuous trading.

Budish: Well, so?

Deanna Dobrowsky: We're really blessed in Canada. I actually know how many marketplaces we have! We have 11. I know which ones are dark.[12] I know which ones are lit.[13] I know their names, and we directly get all of their regulatory feeds. We are blessed with having even more information than you are able to have in the US.

Performing these studies is very difficult. Over the course of a year ago, we started narrowing, looking at what we call the clustering of high order-to-trade ratio data. Because we didn't know what HFT was, because no one seems to know what HFT is. So we reviewed the clusters of data that have a high order-to-trade ratio.[14] We found, as many people now know, that a high order-to-trade ratio isn't necessarily

---

[11] On a lit exchange, such as the New York Stock Exchange, traders can interact with visible prices. The continuous limit order book is a feature of stock and future exchanges across the globe.

[12] At the time of the conference, the dark markets in Canada were Bloomberg Tradebook, Liquidnet, and TriAct Match Now.

[13] At the time of the conference, the lit markets in Canada were Alpha Exchange, Chi-X Canada, CX2 Canada, Lynx ATS, Omega ATS, Toronto Stock Exchange, IMX Select, and TSX Venture Exchange.

[14] Order-to-trade ratio refers to the ratio of orders received by a marketplace compared to the number of trades executed on that marketplace. As the speaker explained in a follow-up, when reviewing trade data, her group was looking for clusters of data that behaved in a similar manner and to then perform research into those clusters.

what everyone thinks of as HFT. It could be proprietary algorithms; it could be regulated market makers. So we looked at the behaviors of the traders that comprise the high order-to-trade ratio group. We're in the process now of refining this information, trying to get to a more narrow group of what HFT is. And we're bringing in academics to look at our data for exactly some of the reasons that Eric Swanson and Eric Budish are talking about. We are going to find different people to perform different reviews and different analyses that might come to different conclusions.

A lot of people jumped for joy when they heard your SEC chair last week say that the SEC might start to disclose trading information publicly.[15] We do that in drips and drabs in Canada. But we will be focusing on HFT-style trading. We will do so in the hope of looking at precisely what you said: at how is it impacting market quality.

There are so many measures of market quality. People turn purple trying to fight for what they think is the best market quality measure. The smartest thing I would think of, along the lines of intelligent regulation, is to get your regulators to seek out the data, review it, have quite a logical (if possible) discussion about it, with as few emotional biases as possible. I would say you probably wouldn't want the regulators to mandate a new form of exchange. But if there are marketplaces that are able to coexist in a Reg NMS system, but which provide a different type of environment, then I think that would be a really great natural experiment.[16]

Lehn: Can you share some patterns in the data you observe in your surveillance efforts?

Dobrowsky: The hot study had certain percentages of trading by high order-to-trade entities.[17] Throughout the remainder of 2012, we tried to refine this data to identify an HFT group. We took high order-to-trade cluster data. We then removed certain trading groups, such as proprietary trading. And just to be clear, in the case of the real-time order and trade data that the Canadian marketplaces are required to report to the IIROC, we know exactly who the broker dealers are. We know exactly the broker dealers who are trading, whether on a dark pool or on a lit pool. And we know who their direct market access clients are. So we're able to break down the

[15] "So, today, I am pleased to announce a new initiative we are launching that is designed to promote a fuller empirical understanding of the equity markets. SEC staff has prepared and assembled resources and data on the SEC's web site focusing exclusively on equity market structure. The new web site should be available as early as next week and will serve as a central location for us to publicly share evolving data, research, and analysis." SEC Chairman, Mary Jo White, Oct. 2, 2013. See full speech: https://www.sec.gov/news/speech/2013-spch100213mjw

[16] Reg NMS (Regulation National Market System) was adopted by the Securities and Exchange Commission in 2005 and introduced 2 years later to further advance the ideals of a national market system. The regulation includes the order protection or trade-through rule, access rule (fair access) to market data including quotations, and rules on sub-penny trading and on market data.

[17] See The HOT Study: Phases I and II of IIROC's Study of High Frequency Trading Activity on Canadian Equity Marketplaces. IIROC, December 12, 2012. http://www.iiroc.ca/Documents/2012/2fb137e3-4371-43bd-b567-59b789a1e4d7_en.pdf#search=HOT%20study

different types of trading entities into various categories, such as by inventory, client/non-client, DMA, and retail.[18] We're able to extract from these clusters the trading entities that you would not consider HFT. Some of the findings are actually a bit surprising, so very high level.

The group we determined to be HFT won't come as a surprise to you. Our preliminary 2012 findings show that HFT-type traders were responsible for 80% of the orders entered on the markets in Canada. They were also part of 35% of the trades. That's not a very high ratio really, right? And coupled with this, I must mention what is sometimes called the Canadian tax.

We're a cost recovery organization. Back in the spring of 2012, we implemented a form of regulatory fee to recover our surveillance and our IT costs, because they're quite significant. So Canadian firms pay a regulatory fee for each message that they send to a Canadian marketplace. That's part of the way in which we recoup our cost. And even with that, as you may know today, we did see order-to-trade ratios early on dip down as you would expect, in response to this regulatory fee that is applied on a per-message basis. But we've actually seen order-to-trade ratios go back up.[19]

I don't know whether these are microstructure or macro issues. Overall, we're seeing lower HFT volumes. Anyway, 15% of the total volume traded were attributing to HFT; and 25% of the total value traded were attributing to HFT.[20] So HFT is a big player in our market. These HFT players are mostly in the US, sending order flow northbound to Canada.[21] Of course, a thorough study is the right way to go.

Lehn: Tom, does FINRA have comparable data?

Tom Gira: Well, not exactly. In the US, we kind of make guesses on what HFT is. There are a lot of statistics that are probably close to what the volume is. In answer to your original question, is HFT a problem or not? Clearly, this discussion shows that there's a lot of positive things about HFT; and there is also a lot of potentially negative things about HFT. And Eric's observations are obviously accurate. I do wonder, though, is that sort of a by-product, or a symptom of a market structure issue, versus strategies that are inherently manipulative or nefarious? A lot of times HFT is lumped in with that type of a discussion. I'm not so sure that's entirely accurate based on how at least I and my staff spend our time.

At FINRA, we spend more time on predatory, opportunistic, and abusive algorithms. Some of those are done by HFT firms; some by prop firms. A lot of them are not in the market at all times. But they are sort of baiting and trying to fish and seeing what's out there in terms of other algos. At FINRA, we launched a cross-market

[18] A typical example of a direct market access client in Canada is a buy-side firm or money manager that is a large, sophisticated institution but is not a broker dealer.

[19] Nothing determined conclusively as to why the order-to-trade ration had gone back up.

[20] Measuring HFT trading in two ways by volume traded and then by total value traded.

[21] Most of the HFT trading volume in Canada is from US-based entities, such as broker dealers or proprietary trading firms.

suite of patterns last year. And we actually have an order auto trail system that allows us to see orders going in and out of the marketplace, from the inception of the order.[22] I think our clients outsource to us because they realize it's a fragmented, very competitive market.[23] We just see quotes and trades and hidden display or lit markets. It looks like one virtual market to us. The reason why we really wanted to be engaged in this cross-market approach is because we were getting a lot of complaints. We were seeing things where participants are consciously spreading their activity around or where you had multiple broker dealers operating simultaneously on the marketplace. About 44% of the Alerts are of the HFT manipulative nature sort, involving trading activity on two different marketplaces.[24] And about 43% of the Alerts are on conduct involving more than one market participant. A lot of times that's one customer who is orchestrating activity through two accounts or two broker dealers who don't know each other. But it's out there, layering, spoofing.[25]

Lehn: Steve, would you like to weigh in?

Steve Wunsch: If you look at HFT as a very much faster and probably more sophisticated version of market making – staying ahead of the flow, trying to make money as professionals in the market – you can get a better understanding of why HFT is really not the problem that people make it out to be. It's true that there's a lot

---

[22] See FINRA 2012 Year in Review here: http://www.finra.org/newsroom/2013/2012-finra-year-review

"In 2012, FINRA implemented comprehensive cross-market surveillance patterns for the markets it regulates (the NYSE and NASDAQ families of markets and the OTC market for listed equities). These patterns address more than 50 threat scenarios and canvas approximately 80% of the listed equities market. FINRA will continue to pursue potential cross-market abuses and refine its surveillance patterns based on new threat scenarios and regulatory intelligence. FINRA also introduced a suite of surveillance patterns to further enhance oversight of trading in non-exchange-listed OTC equities, which will allow FINRA to better review for potential manipulative trading activity, such as frontrunning and marking the close. In addition, as TRACE* has provided increased transparency to the debt markets, FINRA has enhanced its ability to review for potential abuses common in transparent markets, such as wash sales, marking the close and trading ahead. In 2012, FINRA Market Regulation's Trading and Market Making Examination (TMMS) program continued to implement a more risk-based approach to planning and conducting examinations. Thematic and cause examinations focused on trading issues associated with alternative trading systems, information barriers, the SEC's market access rule and amendments to FINRA's order protection rule."

Source: FINRA 2012 Year in Review here: http://www.finra.org/newsroom/2013/2012-finra-year-review

*Trace is the acronym for Trade Reporting and Compliance Engine. According to FINRA, Trace is the "FINRA-developed vehicle that facilitates the mandatory reporting of over-the-counter secondary market transactions in eligible fixed income securities."

[23] FINRA's regulatory clients include the NYSE, NASDAQ, BATS, CBOE, IEX, BOX, and MIAX. See FINRA Regulatory Services: http://www.finra.org/industry/regulatory-services.

[24] A reference to FINRA Alerts or warnings to investors.

[25] Spoofing is defined under the 2010 Dodd-Frank Act as, "the illegal practice of bidding or offering with intent to cancel before execution." Some regulators use the terms "spoofing" and "layering" interchangeably.

of nefarious, I'm assuming, manipulative activity – spoofing, layering, and so on. But all of these activities seem to be very minor versions of old market-making strategies.

Some would like to call them front running. Of course, there has always been a lot of crafty ways that the sell-side tries to keep ahead of the order flow to make money at their jobs. But if you take the net effect of all that HFTs are doing, whether it's considered to be legitimate or nefarious, the net effect of the trading cost is really low.

I know that trading cost analysis has always been sort of a dark art; and it's hard to actually piece together what the trading costs really are. But if you're looking at it in the most simple way, such as a retail investor coming to buy or sell a stock, it really is just the spread that he sees and call that a penny. And it really is just the commission that he pays. Consider Bob Pisani's example earlier of the 1000 shares of IBM that used to cost a lot of money, $500 as he noted.[26] Today, the same customer is only going to pay $8 on the same order, plus the penny a share, which comes to an additional $10. So, overall, it will cost him $18. And whatever murder and mayhem is going on in between the spread, as the HFTs do their thing, is really not relevant.

That's it; the problem with HFT is partly a perception problem and partly a fact of the life of all of those regulatory folks in Washington who would like to try and show us a better way to make life fair. As though the long-term investor needs a better break compared to the short-term HFT!

My view is that we ought to just live with the HFT players, with all of their faults and warts at this point. Their trading costs to the market are as low as they've ever been and actually far, far lower than they've ever been in general for most players. There's just not much to be gained by trying to change the rules or hamper those who are cancelling orders. There's just nothing that I could see that could be gained by that.

Lehn: Some of you have views about Reg NMS and the extent to which that might be the source of some problems in the market structure today.[27]

Wunsch: Funny you should ask. I don't want to call Reg NMS the apotheosis or the epitome of the regulatory direction of the SEC and market regulators, in general. No matter where you come into the market, you will get the best price in the market. But it's by regulatory law that you have to be routed and re-routed until you get the best price, and that's what Reg NMS does. I call it the apotheosis, because I was thinking of how Frank Hatheway started out this morning by talking about how the

[26] See Chap. 4: Integrity of a Marketplace Moderator: Bob Pisani, Correspondent, CNBC.

[27] Reg NMS (Regulation National Market System) was adopted by the Securities and Exchange Commission in 2005 and introduced 2 years later to further advance the ideals of a national market system. The regulation includes the order protection or trade-through rule, access rule (fair access) to market data including quotations, and rules on sub-penny trading and on market data.

goal now of NASDAQ is to preserve alpha.[28] I was just thinking right off the bat of how different that is from the goal of exchanges when they first started. The goal of the New York Stock Exchange's precursor, which originally was the Buttonwood Agreement or, 25 years later in 1817, the New York Stock Exchange Board, was to make as much money as possible.[29] They made their money through a price-fixing cartel and by setting all of the rules in their favor. They were not thinking about preserving alpha for anybody; they had more important things in mind.

I know inclusion is a very popular word and concept these days. But if you think about what they were doing back then, their entire market structure was based on exclusion. The difference between an exchange member and a nonmember was all that really mattered. The members were sworn to each other to preserve that difference and to enhance its value to them, the members, and not to the public. Their goal was not to provide price discovery with integrity or otherwise. Their goal was not to provide capital formation. Their goal was to make money. It was probably the best example in history of Adam Smith's invisible hand. The private interests of profit-seeking people created a structure that wound up creating more capital, and more economic value, to this country and this city than the world had ever seen.

So I find that things like Reg NMS, and the whole modern panoply of rules, have actually been very successful at killing off that old structure. If you wonder why several people have mentioned that the more things change, the more they stay the same and how they talk about how everyone is always unhappy, here's the thing: There is never enough reform for some people; we've always got to do something more! That's because for 80 years, since the creation of the SEC, we've been essentially unwinding the structure that was previously so successful.

That structure is now mostly unwound. Trading costs have been ground down essentially to zero or close enough to zero that we really ought to stop thinking about it anymore or thinking that we can improve it any further. We ought to realize that when we're seeing problems in the market, whether they're perceived in terms of the fairness of HFT, and the SIPs going down.[30] It's because we're actually trying to destroy the structure that was built, and that worked very well, when it was run by human beings.

---

[28] In a follow-up, Wunsch further explained that he was asking why should it be the primary goal of an exchange to preserve alpha. The goal historically of exchanges was to make money for its members, he said, not to preserve alpha. By the same token, he contended, the goal of regulation since the founding of US exchanges has been to destroy profit-seeking by members.

[29] The Buttonwood Agreement, signed by 24 stock brokers outside of 68 Wall Street in Lower Manhattan under a buttonwood tree, on May 17, 1792, created the New York Stock and Exchange Board, now known as the New York Stock Exchange.

[30] "The Security Information Processor (SIP) links the US markets by processing and consolidating all protected bid/ask quotes and trades from every trading venue into a single, easily consumed data feed." Source: Consolidated Tape Association.

More broadly, the NYSE and NASDAQ, at time of writing, each operated a SIP for US stock exchanges, the former showing the best bid and offer for NYSE-listed stocks and the latter showing the NBBO for NASDAQ stocks. These data processors consolidate quote and trade data for stocks listed on their exchanges. The data is then disseminated for a fee to investors, market data providers, and others. NYSE also operated a SIP for options exchanges.

These humans came together and formed a single unified trading network around the NYSE's monopoly which then expanded – through NASDAQ or the over-the-counter market – to bring us the capital formation engine that we once knew until fairly recently. So, yes, Reg NMS is a problem. But it's not because it created high-frequency trading; it's because it's still creating an ongoing regulatory jihad to kill off the market that was really so successful.

Lehn: Eric, any comments on that?

Swanson: No comment (laughter)!

...No, I do, just a quick comment. Obviously Reg NMS has driven a tremendous amount of competition in the industry, and in the exchange industry. I think this as a representative of BATS. BATS existed in the absence of Reg NMS. I wasn't a tremendous supporter of Reg NMS when it was proposed. Nonetheless, we've been operating under the rules of Reg NMS now for the last half a decade. It's a good idea that the commission announced a holistic review of market structure. I do recognize that it will take some time to complete. But it would not be wise for us to go straight to unwinding Reg NMS, without a study to discover the true impact.

Frankly, in response to one of the questions asked earlier about the one single thing you would change about market structure, I would say that it is this one-size-fits-all approach in the regulatory structure today. We've seen it doesn't work so well for all securities all the time. It's encouraging to see the commission moving towards a potential pilot around wider tick sizes in certain instances.[31] More analysis around where we could differentiate, based on the trading characteristics of the security, or the needs associated with capital formation, is a good idea. I hope that comes out of the study.

Lehn: Chairman White last week in a speech indicated skepticism about the one-size-fits-all approach, which is consistent with what you are saying.[32]

Swanson: It's encouraging.

Lehn: Deanna, does Canada have an analogue of Reg NMS; something similar?

Dobrowsky: We do, and it would horrify Steve! We have an exceptionally pure, I'd say, best price model, so we have full depth of book requirements. If it's a better price all the way down the book, anything that's better, you have to hit it if it's on a lit market. You have to connect to every lit marketplace, regardless of the amount of

[31] The pilot eventually was approved by the Securities and Exchange Commission. See *SEC Approves Pilot Program to Assess Tick Size Impact for Smaller Companies.* Press Release. Securities and Exchange Commission. May 6, 2015. https://www.sec.gov/news/pressrelease/2015-82.html

See also *SEC Approves Pilot Program to Assess Tick Size Impact for Smaller Companies.* Center for Financial Stability, May 7, 2015. http://centerforfinancialstability.org/wp/?p=5987

[32] *Focusing on Fundamentals: The Path to Address Equity Market Structure*, speech delivered by SEC Chair Mary Jo White, October 2, 2013, Security Traders Association 80th Annual Market Structure Conference, Washington, DC. https://www.sec.gov/news/speech/2013-spch100213mjw

volume that they trade. And in Canada, it's a topic of discontent for a lot of people that trading entities are required to access all lit markets in order to ensure compliance with the Canadian full depth-of-book order protection model. The sell-side describes itself as a captive consumer because they feel that they are being forced to access these lit marketplaces at costs – both trading and data costs – that they don't think are reasonable.

Given that the theme is price discovery, instead of Reg NMS, let me note that we have the OPR, or the Order Protection Rule, in Canada.[33] The other side of best price is that you are protecting the lit orders that are posted. I actually wouldn't mind understanding from Steve then, if you're not enforcing best price, what's going to make people post in the lit market?

Lehn: It's too bad Craig Lewis from the SEC is not here.[34] He called Friday night to let me know that because of the government shutdown, he would be unable to attend today. But you do have a potential taker to your left there from Canada; maybe she'll take it up?

Dobrowsky: You guys could try it in your market, and then we'll watch it (laughter). If any of you have traded in Canada, you know our stock list is completely different than yours, right? Only one third of the issuers listed on the Toronto Stock Exchange has a market cap of $250 million, or greater. We have a lot of small market cap issuers, and there are liquidity gaps certainly, when trading these small-cap issuers. Not sure if that's caused by market structure or other forces, but definitely it would be of interest.

Lehn: Deanna and Tom, maybe you can tell us about how FINRA and IIROC conduct market surveillance? I know you had mentioned, Deanna, that there's some innovations you've adopted at IIROC. It might be worthwhile, just to understand a little better how you go about it.

Gira: As I said earlier, we're very technology dependent. That 80% I alluded to a while ago, plus all the other data we bring in, it's about 15–20 billion events a day we're processing through our systems. We have around 300 surveillance patterns. Some are more complex than others. If somebody is spoofing or layering, that's a bit more of a complex pattern. But it's just driven by the results of those things. In terms of HFT, we don't spend a lot of time looking at one instance. Say there are dueling algos or one algo is being victimized.[35] In that instance, we're literally looking for thousands and thousands times before that hits our radar screen. When it does, it's fairly pronounced.

---

[33] See The Order Protection Rule, http://www.osc.gov.on.ca/en/Marketplaces_order-protection_index.htm

[34] At the time of the conference, Craig Lewis was chief economist at the SEC and was originally scheduled to join the panel.

[35] The general concept of "dueling algos" or algorithms is described in this piece, Dueling algorithms: If software companies design their algorithms with the sole intention of outperforming each other, the customer can be the loser. Larry Hardesty, *MIT News*. March 18, 2011. http://news.mit.edu/2011/dueling-algorithms-0318

We also look for what we call pivots in the market. Some of these can take place within a sub-second. We kind of base our surveillance by looking at those inflection points. We also will track and see if there are instances of those inflection points. And these give us a learning opportunity to see if they are patterns that aren't working as designed or if there's behavior that we haven't captured in the pattern.

Any regulatory program has to be adaptive and flexible. Because the patterns and the baiting activity, and things like that, are constantly morphing and trying to make themselves look more random – to sort of entice people to take the bait and move the market.

Dobrowsky: Another personal disclosure, I've only been at IIROC for over a year. I worked at TMX group – the company that operates the Toronto Stock Exchange – for about 10 years. It is the main equity marketplace group in Canada. I have observed that IIROC meets on a fairly regular basis with FINRA, so we can share that intelligence and learn from the patterns that FINRA is seeing in trading. There is so much cross-border trading, so much flow that comes north to Canada. Strategies that are being used for trading on equities markets in the US are certainly being used coming northbound.

On the surveillance side, we're trying to get better at storing the data that comes through our feeds. We can use this data effectively for a lot of surveillance, post real-time surveillance, a lot of patterns that you can look for on T-plus-1 or on other post-trade dates.[36] You don't need to perform all the regulatory reviews in real time. Historically, we haven't had a proper warehouse to store all the data that we review in real time. As Eric says, when you've a lot of high-frequency trading, you need to develop IT systems to deal with that as a regulator. For us, that means creating an equity data warehouse that we can access more readily, for post-trade analytics purposes. For me as a policy-maker, that's very helpful. We can use that data quite easily to review post-rule implementation and can do some analysis before we bring forth a rule.

Gira: As we've been talking about equity patterns – options are separate, futures are separate – the SEC's proposed consolidated audit trail starts us down a path we need to get to.[37] As regulators, we also need to look at – I hate to repeat this word – a holistic view of the marketplace with all the asset classes together, rather than sort of looking at them in a balkanized way.

Lehn: Let's shift gears and turn to some of the high-profile technological problems in securities markets the past couple of years, involving systems failures at

[36] Whenever you buy or sell a stock, bond, or mutual fund, there are two important dates of which you should always be aware: the transaction date and the settlement date. The abbreviations T+1, T+2, and T+3 refer to the settlement date of security transactions and denote that the settlement occurs on a transaction date plus 1 day, plus 2 days, and plus 3 days. Source: Investopedia.

[37] *SEC Approves Plan to Create Consolidated Audit Trail.* Securities and Exchange Commission, Press Release, Washington, D.C., Nov. 15, 2016. https://www.sec.gov/news/pressrelease/2016-240.html

exchanges, and problems with order routing at broker dealers. Of course, BATS has had a couple of those, Eric.[38] Do you think that these problems reflect systemic problems related to market structure, or is it just inevitable glitches you get as technology is changing?

Swanson: It's probably somewhere in between. I mean there's some inevitability associated with having technology problems, as we all know and have heard earlier today. But the kind of regulatory scheme associated with technology in our infrastructure could be enhanced. It takes effort to do that. When we have technology failures they tend to get a lot of attention. But they're not as frequent, frankly, as you might think, and they're not all equal. The NASDAQ SIP going down, that was a big deal, no question about it.[39] But when a single exchange has an issue that causes it to have to get out of the market, there's a very good, healthy, self-help mechanism in our marketplace that allows the market to kind of bypass that market while it's having an issue.[40] That works exceedingly well.

We should take a pause for a minute to think about a lot of things that we've actually done to help enhance the resiliency of the market. Reg NMS was in some ways brilliant, injecting the concept of self-help into it. You know we had the Flash Crash of May 6, 2010, which wasn't in and of itself a technology problem.[41] But a lot of remedial measures that flowed from that are helping prevent additional technology problems from having a follow-up effect on the marketplace. Those initiatives are things like the establishment of single-stock circuit breakers, which ultimately led us to limit up, limit down changes in how we handle erroneous executions.[42] Another

---

[38] For example, BATS earliest attempt for its IPO was scrapped after a software glitch sent its shares plunging a fraction of a cent within seconds, when the IPO was originally attempted on March 23, 2012.

[39] *Nasdaq says software bug caused trading outage*, John McCrank, Reuters August 29, 2013. http://www.reuters.com/article/us-nasdaq-halt-glitch-idUSBRE97S11420130829

[40] Under Reg NMS, the best price in the displayed market must be honored. Consequently, there is a mechanism to respond to a situation where that best price is out there but not accessible. So, if a market is having a technical problem, the market might have a quote that a participant can't access. Under Reg NMS, if a repeated attempt by a market participant to access that quote during a single, one second period of time is unsuccessful, the participant can declare "self-help." The participant does this by sending a notice to the exchange it is declaring self-help to. In practice, typically what market participants have done was blast a notification to the street that it has declared "self-help." That allows a participant to immediately start ignoring the quote from that market having a tech problem, until such time as that market publicly acknowledges it is fixed. It might be a barometer of improvement in tech controls in that self-help declarations were much more common when this provision was originally introduced.

[41] The Flash Crash of May 6, 2010, lasted about 36 min, erasing 998.5 points in the Dow Jones Industrial Average and then quickly recouped much of the losses as the various indexes rapidly rebounded in this high-speed, electronic trading phenomenon.

[42] See NASDAQ Frequently Asked Questions: https://www.nasdaqtrader.com/content/MarketRegulation/LULD_FAQ.pdf

is the SEC enactment of the Market Access Rule, which came into effect in 2012.[43] You've also got a proposed regulation, SCI, which I believe will get passed.[44] I'm encouraged that some of the dialog from folks at the commission is taking a fresh look at what was proposed and is about technology problems. But not every single technology problem is the same in terms of its impact. We should be focused on things that are truly critical, making sure that there are appropriate controls and redundancies. You hear a lot of talk now about single points of failure, particularly in the aftermath of the NASDAQ SIP outage.[45] The most recent initiative was Chairman White bringing the SROs all together in Washington.[46] The various work streams coming out of that in many respects intersect with the rulemaking with Regulation SCI.[47]

There's a certain inevitability associated with technology problems. But there are some steps that we can take in the relatively near term to enhance resilience and redundancies, particularly around those single points of failure. I am hopeful that even though we will continue to have some technology problems going forward, we're not going to be talking about them the way we are now.

Lehn: We can point out that the Securities and Exchange Commission is doing better in that regard than the health-care exchange, at least at this point! Deanna, in Canada, have you experienced similar technological issues or not?

Dobrowsky:

Thankfully, not for a while. But they do happen. We were slow to bring in the equivalent of the Market Access Rule that applies in the US.[48] It didn't make us feel warm and fuzzy when, in the middle of proposing it, the Knight Trading incident happened when you already had your Market Access Rule in place.[49]

---

[43] The Securities and Exchange Commission adopted the final version of Rule 15c3-5 on November 3, 2010. See *Risk Management Controls for Brokers or Dealers with Market Access.* Securities and Exchange Commission. https://www.sec.gov/rules/final/2010/34-63241.pdf

[44] Regulation Systems Compliance and Integrity (Regulation SCI) is a set of rules created by the US Securities and Exchange Commission to monitor the security and capabilities of US securities markets' technological infrastructure. The Commission adopted Regulation SCI and Form SCI ("Form") in November 2014.

[45] See footnote 39.

[46] In the week after the 2010 Flash Crash, then SEC Chairman, Mary Jo White, convened a meeting of US exchange officials, and self-regulatory organizations generally, to look at ways to mitigate potentials points of failure in the marketplace officials.

[47] See footnote 44.

[48] See footnote 33.

[49] Aug. 1 stock trading fiasco costs Knight $604 M, USA Today, October 17, 2012. According to the opening paragraph in this AP story: "The Knight Capital Group trading firm said it lost $764.3 million in the third quarter because of a software glitch that flooded the stock market with trades one day in August, causing dozens of stocks to fluctuate wildly." http://www.usatoday.com/story/money/markets/2012/10/17/knight-capital-earnings/1638817/

Rules aren't always everything. Like most regulators globally, we learned a lot from the Flash Crash of May 6, 2010.[50] What might be common sense to a lot of people is that we should write some rules about how firms should better manage risk. And so, like other jurisdictions, we're definitely blessed in Canada. Oftentimes, we get to watch how things play out here in the US and then base our rulemaking on our experience with US regulation.

So we brought in a Market Access Rule, which puts requirements on broker dealers.[51] We have a single-stock circuit breaker concept. We're not moving to a limit up, limit down model.[52] Our single-stock circuit breaker is focused on quite a small group of securities that are in the TSX composite index. We have not mandated the specific volatility thresholds that each marketplace needs to have in Canada.[53] But we have the ability to do that through some rulemaking of the Canadian Securities Administration, our overseeing regulatory body in Canada. Overall, we've responded to the 2010 event through a series of risk management rules. We don't have an equivalent of SCI coming out.[54]

Gira: In some ways we're like a big guinea pig for Canada. If you look at the number of erroneous TRACE complaints that have been adjudicated, there's been a real dramatic decline in that.[55] And since the first half of 2008, and looking at the first half of 2013, there's been an 89% decline in the number of those types of complaints. Since the Flash Crash of 2010, there's been a 55% decline.

A lot of those are more errors that originate with broker dealers, not with the exchanges. But that's sort of a proxy for how the SEC's Direct Market Access Rule has sort of upped the game on the controls.[56] There is still a lot of room for improvement though. We see a lot of one-size-fits-all-type approaches to customers in setting limits.

Swanson: Look at the numbers of self-help declarations.[57] These are not reported, but they are an indication of an exchange having a technology problem. The numbers

[50] See footnote 41.

[51] In Canada, this is National Instrument 23–103 Electronic Trading and Direct Electronic Access; and these rules are also found in the Universal Market Integrity Rules of the Investment Industry Regulatory Organization of Canada (IIROC).

[52] See footnote 42.

[53] In 2016, a mechanism for volatility thresholds was implemented by the Investment Industry Regulatory Organization of Canada (IIROC).

[54] See footnote 44.

[55] TRACE is the acronym for Trade Reporting and Compliance Engine. According to FINRA, TRACE is the "FINRA-developed vehicle that facilitates the mandatory reporting of over-the-counter secondary market transactions in eligible fixed income securities." http://www.finra.org/industry/trace

[56] The Securities and Exchange Commission adopted the final version of Rule 15c3-5 on November 3, 2010. See Risk Management Controls for Brokers or Dealers with Market Access. Securities and Exchange Commission. https://www.sec.gov/rules/final/2010/34-63241.pdf

[57] See footnote 40.

have been steadily coming down year over year as well. I don't know exactly what they are right now, but I would guess it's a small percentage of what they were 4 years ago.

Budish: I completely agree with Eric's position on technology glitches – there's no magic bullet to prevent glitches. It can't prevent programmers from making coding errors. It's inevitable in any system with technology. But I do want to highlight a few ways in which continuous time markets exacerbate the risks of technological glitches relative to discrete time markets.[58]

Continuous time markets give exchange computers a computationally impossible task to perform, which is to keep up with the surge of orders – at times a surge of message traffic – and then disseminate outcomes from that surge of message traffic in real time. Computers are very fast, but they're not infinitely fast. You need to build in some window of time for computers to perform their basic processing and communications functions. A discrete time market in which markets clear once per 100 milliseconds, or once per second, gives exchange computers that window of time to perform their task.[59]

Secondly, there's a race in a continuous time market, and microseconds or even nanoseconds can matter. So optimized code isn't robust code, or it isn't necessarily robust code. No market design reform will prevent the Knight Capital glitch.[60] But you can at least let trading algorithms be written in discrete time. You get information, make decisions, get new information, make decisions – so discrete time is a much more natural approach for algorithms.

When there is a technological glitch, just think back on the Flash Crash.[61] Regulators have an impossible task to perform, to piece together what happened. It took US regulators months to figure out the basic sequence of events that led to the Flash Crash.

Wunsch: I love your idea. I wish I knew you back when we were operating the Arizona Stock Exchange![62] I'd like to ask about this: We've had several SIP errors lately, SIPs going down. I don't recall many times, if ever, that SIPs have gone down before that. And they all seem to be happening now. I don't know whether this is related. I've read and talked to people about how the SIPs have gotten very fast. People are very proud of the fact that they speeded up the SIP. But, they'll never be

[58] See footnote 10.

[59] Ibid.

[60] See footnote 40.

[61] See footnote 41.

[62] Steve Wunsch is the founder of the now defunct Arizona Stock Exchange, an electronic stock exchange based on call auction principles. The headquarters was in New York. A former Kidder Peabody vice president. Wunsch is also known for his expert knowledge of market structure and for his free enterprise outlook.

as fast as the private feeds.[63] This sort of fills in your comment on why the call market is a better choice than the continuous. It just might be that one of the reasons SIPs are going down is simply because they have gotten faster. Put another way, if it isn't a problem yet, then if they were to get ten times faster from here on, or 100 or even 1000 times faster, wouldn't that lead to even greater problems if they do go down? If a fire hose is spewing that kind of data that fast, the faster it gets, the harder it becomes to stay connected and then to get reconnected.

I'm curious if anyone here today even knows the speed of the SIPs? I know at least the OPRA SIP and the NASDAQ SIP have become much faster than they used to be a fairly short time ago.[64] They're all trying to speed up, so that they don't seem to be so unfair compared to the private feeds. Is that a potential problem?

Swanson: I'm not an expert in exactly what happened in the SIP outages. But I don't think there's any evidence to suggest that speed itself was a factor in those outages. There may be some issues at stake around basic controls, say if there's a fire hose of information coming out at you, just having controls in place to make sure that doesn't cause you further problems downstream. I wouldn't characterize that necessarily as a speed problem or a consequence of the SIP, itself, getting faster. I'm not aware of any evidence of it.

Lehn: Does anybody in the audience want to respond to that or raise any other issues about it?

Male Voice: I've been patiently sitting here and listening, not rushing with too much speed! I'm basically in your corner, Eric Budish, in terms of the value of discreteness. We've just gone crazy with speed. I know Joe Rosen, an industry executive, who is in the audience, likes to offer the analogy of 70, 80, and 100 mile an hour cars on city streets. You can get carried away with that. The main value of speed is that it means that something can get there first. And yet, no matter how fast everybody is going, somebody is going to be first; somebody is going to be second. And it has its impact. But we're not benefitting from it. There is a dark side to it once you get to this very high velocity. Whether it's once a second, or once every half a second, it should be calibrated. But once we get into this arms race of speed, the technological cost is enormous. I don't know what the number is. But I know it's enormous.

---

[63] Larry Tabb, writing in the Tabb Forum in December 2016, notes the concept of the consolidated/aggregated market data feed in the US equity markets.

Tabb explains: "Data for the consolidated feed is published by the various exchanges, aggregated by the Securities Information Processors (SIPs), and then distributed to the SIPs' subscribers (either directly or through market data providers). The consolidated feeds historically are slower than exchange direct feeds. While the SIPs have been working on accelerating aggregated data feeds, the process of significantly improving SIP latencies and robustness shifted into overdrive after the August 2013 SIP outage that closed the US equity markets for 3 h. Many market participants believe that if we can reduce SIP latency, it will reduce latency arbitrage and create a fairer and more efficient market. While this is true, eliminating direct feed/SIP latency arbitrage is more complicated than just speeding up the SIP."

[64] OPRA is the acronym for the Options Price Reporting Authority.

Lee Van Slyke [President, Extraordinary Re]: One of the big effects of market regulation and the dreaded SEC (and I'm sorry Craig isn't here) is that we have almost no IPOs coming out at reasonable sizes anymore. And yet we now see crowdsourcing raising a million dollars for a new consumer product. And all they can do is give away samples of the consumer product, because it's illegal to give stock. That seems really unfair to the people who put money up for these new ventures. Is there anything about what you're saying that would lead to either better auctions, or better trading, or more liquidity?

Swanson: Congress has recognized this and has taken some steps in connection with the JOBS Act.[65] It almost goes back to the one-size-fits-all regulation. In general, it doesn't work. I am saying the one-size-fits-all regulation is a bad idea. It remains to be seen whether or not there's a cause/effect here that is associated with what Congress has identified as the problem in bringing emerging companies to the public markets. But Congress is taking steps to ease the burdens of SOX regulation (potentially through its study of this tick pilot) to see whether or not having a wider tick increment might help smaller companies trade better in the public markets.[66]

There's a widely shared perception of a problem. There's some initiative on the hill to take some steps to move away from one-size-fits-all regulation. Congressman Scott Garrett has been active on this front in the House Financial Services Committee.[67]

Andrew Alpert [Rosenblatt Securities]: On the issue of discrete market time, Eric, maybe you could help me out here. I'm not convinced that having a repetitive auction in discrete market time will necessarily lead to better outcomes. The only reason I say that is because my understanding of the continuous marketplace is that there is utility, if you will, in the marketplace for that race to occur. If two liquidity providers are competing to provide liquidity, that brings liquidity to the market more quickly and potentially at better prices.

If you were to move to a discrete market time in repetitive auctions, isn't there a danger that you are actually creating poorer market outcomes at each step along the way? Because there isn't that desire by profit-seeking liquidity providers to really compete to provide liquidity at the best price.

Budish: I would emphasize that profit-seeking liquidity providers in the continuous market are constantly at risk of being picked off by other profit-seeking market

---

[65] Jumpstart Our Business Startups (JOBS) Act https://www.sec.gov/spotlight/jobs-act.shtml

[66] See footnote 31. Referring to a proposed pilot program for trading small-cap stocks in wider minimum increments.

[67] Congressman Scott Garrett (R-NJ, 5th) 2003–2017 chaired the US House Financial Services Subcommittee.

On April 14, 2017, President Donald Trump nominated him to be chairman and president of the Export–Import Bank of the United States.

participants who know the same things they do, who have the same technology, have access to the same information, but who might happen to react a nanosecond faster than they do to some piece of information.

Think about the market for the S&P 500 ETF in New York. Suppose I'm a liquidity provider, a profit-seeking liquidity provider in that market – I'm providing bids and asks in that market–and there's some price signal coming from Chicago, perhaps a jump in price in the Chicago S&P 500 futures market, and then there's a jump in that price in Chicago. As a liquidity provider, I am worried that you're going to pick me off, even if I understand the relationship between futures prices and ETFs just as well as you do and even if I have the same technology you have. Because it's one of me racing to cancel and many of you racing to snipe me, I'm usually going to lose that race. Just one of you has to beat me to the finish line. That's a cost to liquidity providers in the continuous market. In our analysis, it's inevitable that liquidity providers' quotes will become stale. It's built into the continuous market design. It's a flaw of the continuous market design. And because of that flaw, liquidity providers in equilibrium quote wider bid-ask spreads than they otherwise would, and they provide less depth than they otherwise would.

Joe Rosen [President RKA, Inc.]: In full disclosure, I'm certainly with Eric and Steve. But tell me if this makes sense in terms of the logical conclusion, in terms of Andy Brooks' outlook that the more things change, the more they stay the same.[68] I'm surprised we haven't heard about a CLOB today.[69] But to follow your logic, Eric, I'm not saying it's a bad thing, but to make your idea work, you will need at least some sort of CLOB. Mechanisms tied together, which suggests you're moving back to a utility type of model. We're talking specifically about equity markets. Is there some flaw in that logic? How do you make what you want to actually happen? You will have a lot of resistance from people in the industry.

Budish: My first goal is to convince you that it's a good idea. The regulatory and exchange-driven path to implementing the idea is complicated; I freely acknowledge that. Partly because our equity market structure in the US is so fragmented. I think that's the main source of complication with implementing this idea.

What's most productive at this stage in the research is to try to persuade people that it's a good idea. Because the public dialog about high-frequency trading has been pretty misguided. Most of the public dialog about high-frequency trading has been along the line of: is HFT good or evil? That's the completely wrong debate. The right debate is this: HFT firms are self-interested actors, optimizing with respect to market rules. If I can shift the debate to market rules and convince some people that continuous time is a bad market rule, then I'll have done some good, and then we can get into the regulatory nitty-gritty.

---

[68] See Chap. 5: A Trader's Perspective: Andrew M. Brooks, Vice President and Head of US Equity Trading, T. Rowe Price Associates, Inc.

[69] Central limit order book, or CLOB, once proposed by regulators met with industry opposition in the late 1990s and early part of the twenty-first century.

Wunsch: I want to say one quick thing about the regulatory side as it relates to the CLOB. I don't know if people have heard of the SEC's historical website?[70] It's a wonderful place to visit; you can learn everything about the SEC. On this website, there's an interview with Ralph Saul, who was actually at the agency in charge of writing the SEC's Special Study of Securities Markets, released in 1963, and that's 50 years ago this year.[71] It was sort of the precursor of everything that led to Reg NMS, the CLOB debate, and all that.[72] In that interview, Saul was asked, "do you regret anything," and he said, "yes." He regretted that they pushed competition for competition's sake on the NYSE. He thinks, in retrospect, we would have been better with the utility model.[73] And this interview was back in the early 2000s, before high-frequency trading really took off. He thought that the competition for competition's sake that the SEC went with was a mistake. He would have gone with the utility model.

Gary Katz: Eric, it's a great idea you've raised, certainly one that deserves more discussion. The ISE, as an options exchange, is not dealing with 3000 securities; we're dealing with 400,000 securities.[74] And our market makers are what you would think of as the liquidity providers, the high-frequency trading liquidity providers. We've asked our market makers whether we should slow the orders coming in, to give them time to update their quotes. In this way, there isn't the opportunity for that arbitrage as people try to pick them off. And time and time again, they've answered no.

It's an interesting perspective that you're trying to protect that liquidity provider. But it may create more of a problem for them; there may be unintended consequences associated with the idea. Nevertheless, I certainly encourage greater discussion.

Budish: It's important to be humble in proposing new market designs. Part of the reason for proposing frequent batch auctions is to minimize the scope for unintended consequences.[75] These are at intervals, so that most market observers won't notice the difference between frequently conducted batch auctions and continuous time limit order books. And there have been unintended consequences associated with the continuous market design. But I freely acknowledge that it is the unintended consequences that should keep us up at night when discussing any market structure reform. As for some of the proposals discussed in the context of HFT, like minimum resting times, you don't have to think very hard about what the conse-

[70] Securities and Exchange Commission Historical Society. http://www.sechistorical.org/

[71] Ralph Saul is listed in 1964 on the historical website, as Director, Division of Trading and Markets at the Securities and Exchange Commission.

[72] See footnotes 16 and 69.

[73] Example of this "utility" model would be the original AT&T entity created by the US government.

[74] The International Securities Exchange (ISE) www.ise.com/about-ise/

[75] See footnote 3.

quences of some proposals would be to realize that they be very negative. With frequent batching, we've subjected it to rigorous academic analysis and have been speaking about the idea to whomever will listen. And I believe that Bob Schwartz has been speaking about the idea to whomever will listen, too.[76] That said, I completely agree that it's important to be humble about unintended consequences.

Lehn: And with that last comment, we can conclude and thank the panel.

[76] Referring to Professor Robert Schwartz's widely known research, proposals, and support for a call market.

Chapter 7
Invited Editorial Comment: Equity Trading in the Fast Lane—*The Staccato Alternative*

Robert A. Schwartz and Liuren Wu

"Competition is good and we want it. (Right on!) Competition keeps prices down, profits in check, and innovation vibrant. (Absolutely!) Competition is fun. (It sure is, if you mean the World Series, Super Bowl, Stanley Cup playoffs, or a kid's game of musical chairs.) Competition should be our goal, our mantra! Whoa, slow down a millisecond. Now you are carrying this too far, too fast."

Since the Congressional Securities Acts Amendments of 1975, intensifying competition has been a key government objective for the equity market, and it remains center stage in the SEC's Order Handling Rules (1997), Regulation Alternative Trading Systems (1999), and Regulation National Market System (2005). These regulations, combined with formidable technology developments, have transformed the markets.

The New York Stock Exchange's commanding dominance in its market has been broken. Back in the 1990s, more than 80% of the order flow for listed stocks was directed to the NYSE, but now the Big Board's market share has fallen to less than 30%. The Nasdaq marketplace has also been massively reengineered, and today its dealer market is playing a far less dominant role. The USA currently sports 13 stock exchanges and more than 40 alternative trading systems (ATSs). What are the consequences?

Reprinted with permission from Invited Editorial Comment: Equity Trading in the Fast Lane–The Staccato Alternative, Schwartz, R., and Wu, L., the *Journal of Portfolio Management*, Spring 2013.39.3:3-6.

R. A. Schwartz (✉)
University Distinguished Professor, Zicklin School of Business, Baruch College/CUNY, New York, NY, USA

L. Wu
Zicklin School of Business, Baruch College/CUNY, New York, NY, USA

© Springer Nature Switzerland AG 2019

R. A. Schwartz et al. (eds.), *Market Integrity*, Zicklin School of Business Financial Markets Series, https://doi.org/10.1007/978-3-030-02871-8_7

The good news is that commissions and exchange fees have fallen sharply, spreads have tightened, and in at least some opinions, market impact costs have declined.

But not all of the news is good. The markets have fragmented not only spatially but also temporally. Time is fractured by today's super-fast electronic trading platforms, which handle quote changes and deliver trades within tiny fractions of a second. On the other side of the coin, preprogrammed computer algorithms fire participant responses into the market, making and even implementing trading decisions almost instantaneously. This has introduced a new fragility to the markets. On this score, the flash crash of May 6, 2010, was a wake-up call.

What can be done to ameliorate this fragility? In this piece, we call attention to the unrelenting competition for speed: the competition between trading firms to get there first when placing or cancelling orders and the competition between market venues to accommodate customers by supplying the speed they crave. And we offer a suggestion for defusing the fragility: transform what has become a hyper-continuous market into staccato trading. But we are getting ahead of our story.

7.1 Competition Is Not A Simple Matter

Enhancing competition in the equity markets is not a simple matter. Regulate them in one way, and unintended consequences occur in other ways. Take the trade-through rule, for example. This rule, a key component of the SEC's Regulation NMS (enacted in 2005), was largely purposed to improve the fairness of order handling and to strengthen competition between alternative trading venues. The rule stipulates that a better quote from a fast (read "electronic") market could not be traded through but allows quotes from a slow (read "human intermediated") market to stay unprotected.

The result? The NYSE was forced to develop an electronic trading platform. Concurrently, it has become a good deal easier for various alternative trading venues to capture order flow. As a result, the market has become far more fragmented, and this fragmentation has given further impetus to the development of high-frequency, algorithmic trading.

Complications concerning the regulation of competition arise largely because there are two distinctly different markets: the market where orders meet and are translated into trades and the market where trading venues meet as they compete for orders (i.e., the market for markets). *Intra*-market competition pertains to competition within the flow of orders (limit orders, market orders, orders with special conditions, and so on). *Inter*-market competition plays out as a competition between alternative trading facilities, all fighting for a larger slice of the order flow. There is a trade-off between the two. Let the markets consolidate to encourage competition within the order flow, and a successful venue gains monopoly power; encourage competition between alternative trading facilities, and the order flow fragments.

Competition within the order flow, if handled properly, can be an effective way to achieve more efficient price discovery. The big question is can good price formation be achieved in a fragmented market? Electronic linkages may tie disparate facilities together, but order flow cannot be fully consolidated between multiple venues that maintain separate books. A secondary priority rule (e.g., time, size, or pro rata) cannot be imposed across different books. Complex orders cannot be displayed and easily integrated into the order flow in the segmented marketplace. With 13 exchanges and 40 plus ATSs operating in the USA, both reasonably accurate price discovery and sufficiently complete quantity discovery have become more difficult to achieve. And there is more: competition does not occur in terms of price alone. Speed also matters.

7.2 The Speed Game

In continuous market trading, high-frequency trading (HFT) firms fight fiercely in a race to enter or withdraw their orders ahead of others. Consequently, the venue that offers the most speed gains a strong competitive advantage over its rivals in the market for markets. In the non-electronic markets of the past, speed was measured in seconds, minutes, or more. Today it is measured in sub-seconds—milliseconds down to microseconds. We are rapidly approaching the speed of light. Has this competition gone out of control?

In economic theory, immediacy of consumption can enhance consumer utility, and values are higher when trades are consummated on a more timely basis. This certainly is the case for equity markets where, given their immediacy needs, natural buyers and sellers put much value on low latency. But a latency-induced utility loss is negligible once we get down to a 1-second tick of the clock. Simply put, once a 1-second frequency has been reached, where does the value of a further sub-second reduction in latency lie for a fundamental investor?

Price discovery is another major role for a market center. Active trading better reveals an underlying security's equilibrium valuation, and low latency can potentially deliver faster price discovery. This advantage also has a limit. If fundamentals do not change as fast, then hyper-fast order posting and trading may no longer speed up price discovery. On the contrary, it may predominantly add jitter to market prices. There is an old saying: "Think before you act." When trading proceeds faster than the blink of an eye, thinking can no longer precede trading. At that speed, thinking must be relegated to preprogrammed computers, and we know where this can lead: to a flash crash. Put it this way: once the market reaches breakneck speeds, faster is not better.

The current use of maker–taker pricing with rebates bestows a special value on speed. Limit orders generally provide liquidity, whereas market orders generally take liquidity. Given that, much can be said for charging lower commissions to "makers" (those who place limit orders) than to "takers" (those who submit market orders).

With maker–taker pricing, however, limit order commissions are not just lower. They are negative, in that they involve a rebate. Not surprisingly, at least in hindsight, this pricing structure has introduced competition to snare the rebates. Many HFT participants submit limit orders, not to buy or to sell shares for fundamental reasons but to capture tiny rebates per share from a very large number of trades. Competing successfully in this arena requires lightning-fast, computer-driven speed—fast, strategic trading decisions, rapid-fire order submissions and cancellations, and quick position flips after trades are realized and rebates captured. As a consequence, there are questions concerning maker–taker's effect on the provision of meaningful liquidity for fundamental investors and on the efficiency of price discovery for the broad market.

When sub-second latency reductions neither add utility for fundamental investors nor enhance price discovery for the broad market, alternative venues that compete in the market for markets by offering low latency no longer contribute to social welfare. On the contrary, they create an arms race that imposes heavy costs on the players and sometimes imposes devastating effects on society. An enormous amount of capital was spent to achieve the technological feat of handling orders, delivering information, and consummating trades with microsecond precision. The result of this spending? A system that, while generating smaller commissions and narrower bid–ask spreads, can obfuscate price discovery and at times completely break down.

Moreover, when the high-frequency trading shops go all out in building their technology infrastructures and co-locating their machines with the exchanges, their objective is no longer to serve as effective intermediaries between natural buyers and sellers but to win the high-frequency race by squeezing in front of one another to pick off orders at advantageous prices, grab rebates, and run away faster than everybody else when they sense that their own orders are mispriced. That is why a seemingly active market with low commissions and narrow spreads can, at the snap of a finger, disappear in a flash crash. In such an environment, natural buyers and sellers have insufficient assurance of receiving reasonably efficient executions. Instead, they are continuously subjected to rip-offs. Inferior price and quantity discovery are the result, discouraging broad public participation in the markets.

7.3 Stepping in Front of Others

High-frequency trading algorithms interact with one another in dynamically changing ways, with consequences that are difficult to understand and virtually impossible to predict. One thing is immutable, however. It does not matter how fast the average participant is. Only one thing counts: being first. Let order deliveries speed up by an average of 10 microseconds. As long as arrival times can be clocked with microsecond precision, only one person will come in first. The gold medal will not be awarded to the player who best translates fundamental information into share values but to the participant who happens to be fastest—the fastest to grab an order and the fastest to run away and avoid being grabbed.

In this high-frequency race, fundamental investors are no longer served. Prices, rather than being discovered with reasonable accuracy, are more apt to be contaminated by stuffing, bluffing, layering, and any other scheme that can mislead customers. After repeated losses, customers may figure out that something unsavory is happening and start to complain, and the SEC has been busy banning certain identified schemes as illegal. Nevertheless, much as viruses mutate from flu season to flu season, as old schemes are banned, new variants appear.

As long as coming in first remains a goal, the drive for ever-faster speed will continue unabated until faster is just not possible, because the markets have reached the speed of light. By then, yet more money will have been spent on development costs, and more fundamental investors will have been disadvantaged.

Something must be done, not to constrain the players per se but to improve the system within which they compete. Is it possible to steer the market toward providing better liquidity and sharper price discovery for natural customers? Alternative proposals have been put forth. One, for instance, would require that an order stay on the book for a minimum amount of time before it can be cancelled.

We have a better suggestion. To achieve an environment that fosters sharper price discovery and more robust quantity discovery, we propose a procedure that uses the time clock very differently. We call this procedure *staccato trading*.

7.4 Staccato Trading

Just as government has established a minimum price tick (currently 1 cent for most stocks), it should set a minimum time tick: 1 s for instance. This would transition the hyper-continuous market into staccato trading. With staccato trading, orders accumulate within the second, and transactions occur at the end of the second, throughout trading hours. During the second, all matched and crossing orders are held for simultaneous execution at a single price, set at the end of the second according to a call auction-clearing algorithm.

In the days of yore on the NYSE trading floor, a specialist paused trading whenever activity suddenly heated up for a stock, and it was not possible, with any kind of meaningful accuracy, to determine a reasonable price or implement a secondary priority rule of order execution. During the halt, a specialist assessed floor traders' collective pressures to buy and to sell shares and determined a more orderly clearing price. That procedure was, in effect, a call auction. Today, a call auction procedure is used to reopen a market after a stock-specific trading halt or a marketwide circuit breaker.

The call uses the time clock differently than continuous trading does. In the call, trading is periodic. The clearing price (only one such price is produced) reflects the assessment of the collective set of submitted orders. This, in our opinion, is a properly produced price discovery. Just as an artfully cooked meal contrasts with fast food, so too does a call auction's single price contrast with a flock of noisy values that primarily reflect not fundamental information but the chance sequence of order arrivals from stealth competitors who seek to step in front of one another in a far too noisy and at times chaotic environment.

Defusing a hyper-continuous market is not a simple task, however, and of course the devil is in the details, especially in an environment comprised of multiple trading venues.

Should staccato trading be a requirement for all trading venues? Yes, with across-the-board regulation stipulating a minimum time tick. Who would provide the liquidity in a staccato trading environment? Designated market makers could play this role, much as they have in the past. Could Regulation NMS's trade-through rule still be applied? We think this would be possible, if markets want it. Can various venues' time clocks be synchronized with sufficient accuracy? Yes.

Further details will undoubtedly arise: whether the books are open as they build, for instance, and whether orders can be cancelled within the second. Questions such as these could potentially be left to the individual markets. But where there is a will, there might well be a way. The whole idea of staccato trading is not to slow down transactions per se but to diffuse the arms race among high-frequency trading venues. We wish to incent genuine liquidity providers, such as designated market makers, and to refocus the market back to the two fundamental goals of a marketplace: reasonably accurate price discovery for the broad market and reasonably complete quantity discovery for natural buyers and sellers.

7.5 Slow Down, You Crazy Child

By all means, let orders and trading venues compete. There is much that vibrant competition can deliver when it is carried out in a constructive way. But competition is not, in and of itself, a be all and end all, and strengthening competition should not be a mantra. Although competition to be the fastest is fine in sports, it is not the equity markets' ultimate goal. Good price and quantity discovery are what we need. As Billy Joel cries out in his song *Vienna*, "Slow down, you crazy child."

Printed by Printforce, the Netherlands